Praise for Paul Tobey

"If you are not afraid to change your life, to get unstuck, to become self-motivated, then Paul Tobey is who you need to know. See results in your business immediately. Paul Tobey is a Change Agent, and somehow is able to accurately pinpoint in me what needs changing, to what, and how. Did I say immediate results?" July 31, 2012

Brian O'Dea Author of Best Selling Book "High" Random House Publishing

"As a committed "life-long learner" I have taken a lot of courses in both personal and professional development. I highly recommend Paul Tobey and Training Business Pros as the best value and most intensive learning experiences available. The Advanced Internet Marketing course was probably one of the best investments I have made in myself – the training gave me cutting-edge information that most people don't know along with valuable tools and techniques. As a consultant I was able to successfully implement these strategies for my clients and this knowledge helped me secure a very lucrative contract. The course has more than paid for itself in a very short period of time. I have also been able to use the techniques I learned from the Train the Trainer course to become a much stronger presenter and allow me to continue to build credibility as an expert." June 13, 2011

Nancy Mayer Globe and Mail

"Paul Tobey is very knowledgeable when it comes to Internet Marketing. By attending his seminar once I was able to double my site's traffic in less than 6 months. And this is considering I was already getting a significant amount of traffic. Paul has also helped me a great deal with public speaking and personal development. I highly recommend Paul and his seminars to everyone who wants to learn and become an expert in their own field." July 26, 2012

Jean Cote

"I attended the Train the Trainer program offered by Paul in the fall of 2011. I had signed up for it 14 months earlier, and kept putting it off. Even when I got there, I was totally unprepared for the experience. I have thought of myself as a competent public speaker since I was a teenager, and am comfortable in front of a crowd, but the skill set that I gained in the 3 days of intensive training moved me light years ahead in my abilities to train. I used some of the techniques I learned the following day in classes I teach at the college, and was amazed at how much better the learning experience was for my students. They were more engaged, and responsive. I even tried some of the techniques which I personally believed would never work in a classroom environment, just so I could say I had tried them. They worked better than a charm. I would HIGHLY recommend anyone who is serious about being able to help others through training, to attend this program. It is WELL worth the price!" July 26, 2012

Robert Pilling Lawrence Kinlin School of Business, Fanshawe College

"If you truly want to get to the top of your game in business then you have to get Paul on your side. He is a true expert in business training and internet marketing." August 10, 2012

Diamond Fernandes

"Paul was the reason I got involved professionally in the internet marketing business. He's an inspirational person with great knowledge and a higher then normal integrity. I always look forward to his next training because I know what he teaches is the next big thing that I must know about. Thank you, always grateful! August 17, 2012

Chris Violetis"

"Paul Tobey's has amazing insight in the world of marketing and promotion, have attended numerous and events and have had great engaging conversation on social media and networking principles that work!" August 7, 2012

Jim Pagiamtzis

"Paul is an amazing coach and trainer. He effectively communicates complicated information in a way that anyone can learn. His courses are effective at helping ordinary people learn highly difficult concepts. After taking Paul's courses I was able to create multiple WordPress websites that have brought in thousands of new visitors a month and new sales for my business." August 5, 2012

Joseph Shaw

"I highly recommend Paul Tobey's Train the Trainer program. It is only one of the phenomenal training experiences I have enjoyed through Paul's company, Training Business Pros. This experience has definitely improved my skills as an entrepreneur." August 2, 2012

Bruce Langford Author

"I attended several training workshops taught by Paul including Internet Marketing and Train the Trainer. He is an SEO expert and keeps current with latest internet strategies and trends. He is an effective speaker/presenter and keeps audience enrolled and engaged. I learned a lot from him and highly recommend his training programs." July 31, 2012

Albert Ramsay

"Paul Tobey is extremely knowledgeable in the world of Social Media Marketing. His diligence and commitment is a true testament of this willingness to go the extra mile. Paul at Training Business Pros, is my coach for launching my own hair salon training courses. Paul Tobey is highly recommended for any internet marketing related courses, and coaching." July 31, 2012

Dee Sarwan

"I took Paul Tobey's Train the Trainer program in 2009. Paul delivered excellent training which provided me with the tools to run my own workshops. Paul knows how to get the best out of people." July 26, 2012

Dale Choquette, CLC, MSLC, ACG, ALB

"One of the biggest problems I see affecting businesses and organizations now is the critical need to improve their training methods. With the looming retirement of so many of their baby-boomer leaders and managers, most organizations are at a loss to find ways to quickly and effectively train their replacements to take over needed responsibilities. Paul Tobey's training methods work. He quickly enrolls and engages his audience so that they learn more than they expected faster than they thought possible. His approach works no matter what you are teaching. His classes are informative, inspirational,

and, if you apply his approaches, enriching. Sign-up for one today!"
July 26, 2012

Trevor McAlpine

"I would definitely recommend Paul Tobey's 2 day SEO and Social Media Training Seminar. The formulas and techniques I have acquired will not only benefit me in my current profession but will be solid stepping stones in any business direction I may decide take in the future. He offers effective techniques to utilize social media, as well as a profound understanding to SEO and the importance it has. Paul's presentation style is highly engaging and enthusiastic and his knowledge is prosperous. Thank you Paul!!!" June 17, 2011

Megan Hooper

"Paul's trainings have been an integral part of our business. Having been a student of Paul's and getting to know him on a personal level over the years, I have watched as he has helped others increase their profits and client lists through his coaching and intensive courses. He does whatever he can to ensure this students are benefiting from their education and implementing what they have learned so they can reach their goals. He is creative and consistently striving to give his students more! Quite frankly for the amount of information and coaching he offers, the value he offers far outweighs the price of his courses! Thank you Paul, for all of your mentorship!" July 27, 2011

Michelle Tavares Albert and York Inc.

"I would recommend Paul's work and courses to anyone who is challenged by Internet Marketing . To say that I learned a lot from Paul would be a major understatement and his work helped me significantly increase revenues for my company , which is a Business Financing firm . Feel free to call or email me anytime for more info." March 3, 2011

Stan Prokop 7 Park Financial

Suggestology

How to Get What You Want By Asking the Right Questions

.

By Paul Tobey

Training Business Pros a division of Pilgrim Productions Incorporated

A Division of Pilgrim Productions Incorporated
Toronto, Ontario M2K1Y1

For information about special discounts and bulk purchases, please contact us at: 1-877-790-PROS (7767)

ISBN: 978-1-62209-278-9

To Nancy

For years of support, I am truly grateful

Contents

Foreward

This is much more than a business book. Yes, it is intended to get you business results. However, the way those results will come about and what you will be asked to do to get those results is likely different from anything you've heard about, read about, or talked about before.

If you have created a goal for yourself and have not yet achieved it, or have yet to arrive at the place you want to be in, then read and implement the strategies within this book.

I have implemented every single strategy that I'm going to talk about and the results have been wealth in life and in business that has been fantastic, fun-filled, and action-packed.

What kind of life do you want? Do you want to do and continue to do the same things you are doing now? If so, then you might want to put this book back on the shelf. Walk away.

If you want new things, new adventure, ultimate experiences, wealth, and business success, then study this book from cover to cover. I personally guarantee every single strategy contained within it.

There are many practical and professional development strategies that will be talked about and there are an equal number of personal development tips and techniques to help you implement those strategies effectively.

Most books focus on one or the other, but not both. My personal belief is that professional development and personal development cannot exist without each other. Yes, you must know the "how-to". But "if how-to's were enough we'd all be skinny, rich and happy."[1] Since "how to's" are only one part of the equation, you will need to learn, digest, and implement certain success rules to achieve your desired outcome.

Suggestology is a how-to strategy that relies on certain irrefutable laws. As a marketing strategist I have learned that Suggestology is the most effective way to communicate with people because it connects directly with how they make decisions. How do most people make decisions? Based on how they feel.

Suggestology is the language and the communication system that uses "feeling" as its fuel. The medium that you use to connect with people and market your business is a mechanism, but that mechanism will not work if the message you are delivering is ineffective. You must communicate the one thing that people need to make a decision in your favor, and that comes with the ability to feel something.

I am excited for you, for I know what will happen to your life when you are open to learning and accept the guidance within these pages.

[1] If How-To's Were Enough, We Would All Be Skinny, Rich and Happy! *by Brian Klemmer*

Introduction

Show me somebody who doesn't make mistakes, and I'll show you someone who just watches television.

People as a general rule don't want to be caught unprepared, to fail. They're afraid to fall down or to look like they don't have answers. Therefore, they conclude that the best way to avoid those things is by never stepping out on a journey of discovery— the very journey that would provide them preparation for risk, soaring success, and the answers they seek. Does this sound familiar?

I'm not knocking you. It makes sense. People avoid journeys for many seemingly logical reasons. One is that they don't know how to get where they want to go. That's fair. More than that, they don't know how to learn where it is they'd like to end up.

Enter this book. I've taken tremendous strides forward in my life as a result of learning through Suggestology and the art of discovery. Now, you can, too.

What is Suggestology?

It is the art of learning through discovery—learning while doing. The purpose of Suggestology is to enhance growth by tapping into the power of suggestion. It has changed my life, and it has helped me change thousands of others' lives who have attended my seminars and bought my training resources.

Suggestology teaches you to tap into the subconscious mind and its natural ability to absorb information. Many speakers and presenters interrupt the learning process by delivering steady streams of data without a break. Bad move. When the mind is not engaged and active, it cannot learn and absorb information effectively. The power of suggestion keeps the mind open and active.

Interestingly enough, the discovery process is something that most people avoid. Surely everyone must know that you can't discover anything unless you do *something*.

So, strap on an open mind and allow me to take you back to the beginnings of my learning processes. By keeping your mind open, you'll have the opportunity to learn from my mistakes, avoid the pitfalls, and get to where you're going faster than ever.

Chapter 1—Leggo Your Ego

When I turned 16, I got my driver's license. I felt it would give me the freedom to explore the world with more freedom. I had saved up about $400 working for my cousin Carl's landscaping company. Even though it was backbreaking work six days a week and 16 hours a day, I kept my eye on the image of hauling around town in my own automobile and all the joys that that entails. It motivated me. I wanted to show everyone how great I was now that I was 16—it's a pretty normal response to turning that age, as I understand.

Anyways, Carl told me that his brother was asking $500 for a car up in Kitchener, which was likely negotiable. It turned out to be a 1974 AMC Gremlin. The car had been stored in a garage, and the brother told me that it wasn't running and would take a bit of mechanical workmanship to get it running. It was rusted. To anyone else it would have been a horrid sight; to me, it was my baby—okay, maybe a baby who needed some TLC.

The little Gremlin was my own freedom machine. How could I not love it?

We towed the car 40 miles from Kitchener to my home in Brantford Ontario and parked it in the family driveway. The very same day I began to sand down the rust spots, fill them in with Bondo and then sand down the Bondo to make a smooth surface. I can still smell the Bondo. (We never thought of wearing things like dust masks.)

I worked every day on the car for several months. My brother pitched in and helped with the mechanics, and we got it running pretty quickly.

I got one of my dad's friends to paint it fire engine red—the same colour, you'll remember, as Starsky and Hutch's Ford

Torino. It was a bold statement to be sure, but something was still missing.

A couple of friends from high school came over and we looked at the car for quite some time, trying to decide what it needed in order to really stand out and be complete. At first we thought that a white stripe, the same as on Starsky and Hutch's car, would do it. But then we thought maybe that would be too obvious, and we didn't want to feel like copycats. So my friend Richard suggested painting flames on the side.

Flames? I thought.

Richard's dad was a bit of an artist and could do it for free. Free was the right price, and I agreed. I couldn't wait to see the orange and red flames flowing up the side of my car and showing it off to everybody. I thought I would be the coolest guy in town.

As soon as the flames were painted, I immediately regretted the decision. Sadly, I didn't have the energy or the money to change it. About two weeks later, while driving home from the pizza place, I got pulled over by the cops. Did I forget to mention that this car was loud? You could spot it from 100 miles away.

It had appeared to the police that I rounded a corner a little too fast and, after checking my driver's license, they demanded to meet my father. How could I refuse?

They followed me to my house. After attending a fifteen-minute chat with my dad about how I was racing around town in the "splashy" car, how they knew what cars "like that" did to the minds and feed of "boys like your son". They basically told him to tell me to keep my lead foot off the pedal because they'd be watching. In the end, I don't think they liked the car.

About a week after the incident with the police, I was coming out the back door of my high school after band practice and noticed that one of my band friends was being picked on by a couple of kids—you know the type: big, brash, caveman-like. I was a shy kid and not much for confrontation. I walked quickly to my car and, as I was leaving, for some strange reason I stopped. Then, I leaned out of the car and yelled out, "Hey! Leave him alone!"

They weren't being physical with him, at least from my perspective, but they were definitely making fun of him. Well, as soon as I yelled, they stopped what they were doing and promptly rushed over to mine. Before I could do anything, one of the boys had reached inside my window and began assaulting me, I, of course, put the car into gear and hit the pedal to the metal, scared as anything.

The next day, I drove to school as inconspicuously as I could in a Gremlin with flames shooting down either side of the paint job, hoping I wouldn't run into the thugs again. Sure enough, the bullies had no trouble finding me. They had been waiting across the parking lot.
I parked. Looking in my review mirror, I saw them—two of them—weaving through the parked cars on a mad dash towards me. *Hurry*, I told myself. But, of course, when your mind wants your body to hurry, sometimes your body does anything but. I fumbled with my book bag. As I left the car, I dropped my keys and then quickly dipped down to scoop them back into my hands.

I heard big, heavy boots on asphalt approaching me.

I was too late.

A solid flash sparked up the left side of my face and everything went bright. Ouch. As I fell my book bag flung away from me. I rose to retrieve it, holding my arms up against the two assailants.

The boys had other plans. One of them lunged at me and I, still woozy from the first hit, was in no mind frame to be Bruce Lee. He grabbed my arms and yanked them behind my back. I realized I was in real trouble. I struggled against the boy but the other one leapt out and struck me in the head.

I went down. The other boy held me back up. I got it in the stomach. Again in the stomach. The ribs. The face. Things got hazy.

I wondered if the boys would stop before I died—and this thought sent a jolt of adrenaline through my body. I leapt away from the boy who had taken up my arms and managed to wrangle free of him. Then, I ran.

Several students had noticed what was going on. I heard them yell at the kids to stop. As I approached the doors to the school, the kids turned away.

The principal met me at the door; he must have heard the ruckus. At the office, the staff assured me they knew exactly who those kids were. They asked if I wanted to go home. I, sitting with my head in my hands, said no. Truth be told, I didn't want to be outside anymore.

As I left the office and chucked my bag into my locker, my ears perked. Big, heavy boots.

I spun around and brought my hands up to block the fist coming at me, but its force sent me sprawling to the ground. My head bounced off the floor. I saw stars. As I was on the ground, it felt as if oversized vipers were attacking me, the heavy boots striking my sides and my face. This time, I was sure they wouldn't stop.

The boys left me in a pool of blood once a student had ran and got some teachers to confront them. The nurse's office called an ambulance and took me to the hospital to stitch up my face, look after my cracked tooth, and take a look at the serious bruising on my head and over my body.

After all was said and done, I was tremendously worried that it would happen again. I mean, I knew that I was safe for at least six months, as the boys both got a six-month jail sentence as well as having been expelled from school. Yes, the beating was that bad.

But the punishment didn't just scar me physically. I went out less. I talked less. I avoided confrontation. After that incident, people often told me that I did not speak or communicate enough. I was scared. If two strangers could do this, just because I yelled out at them to stop beating on somebody, who else was capable of such a thing? And how stupid was I to have yelled out at them while I was driving a car that made me one of the most recognizable people in my city?

I held on to that fear for many years.

After such a bad experience in expressing my individuality, I receded into myself, and even my close friends were worried that I was not the same person. Being attacked verbally, physically, and emotionally had changed me. If it hadn't been for those big flames, most of it wouldn't have happened.

Was it my car that caused all of this? Was it my attitude? Did I attract this somehow?

Not long after this incident, my Gremlin was stolen from the back parking lot of the restaurant where I worked delivering pizzas and playing the old piano for $3.50 an hour. The two young men who stole it were chased by the police for several kilometers before they wrapped my car head-on into a telephone pole. Apparently the driver was hurt quite badly and broke his leg in several places. Later that day at the police station, I overheard one of the cops say, "Hey, did you hear we got that pesky gremlin off the road? You know—the one with the flames?"

Lesson - You've Been Programmed

From the time a baby is born until they are seven years old, they are said to be in *the imprint period* . At this age you cannot psychologically filter anything; whatever you hear or see is imprinted on you as if it were the truth—it becomes your belief system. Most of what you see and hear is from the people who are closest to you, namely your parents, siblings and teachers. Therefore, whatever they believe is what you end up believing. It becomes your truth. What they believe is not necessarily the truth, but their truth.

After that until your middle teens, you're in *the modeling period.* You begin to understand that you are an individual. You are still highly impressionable and believe mostly what those around you believe, but you begin to break away by modeling yourself after those who you admire.

In my case, it manifested in me wanting to be different and to have freedom. My Gremlin was the physical manifestation of those wishes. Sadly, it seemed to attract a ton of trouble. It got me beat up, harassed by police, and the car was stolen. My ego was battered by learning that you shouldn't stand out for your ego's own sake. That's kid stuff that leads to trouble.

Standing out for the sake of ego will always bring problems. The mind is the ego. When the ego tries to exert itself, nothing good can come of it.

The more you try to separate yourself from others through ego, the more you will see the pain of life. It usually takes several years to see this; indeed, some people never see it. Only compassion, caring, giving, love, and similar positive heartfelt emotions can make you feel good. You can never feel good for long by dominating others.

Only when you begin to see that your ego is the source of all problems in your life can you truly live peacefully. All forms of dominance and egotistical behavior attract problems. The ego attracts other people with ego. Like attracts like. This is an irrefutable law of the universe. When you seek to dominate other people, other people will show up in your life to dominate you. This is how wars are started.

There are varying degrees of war. You can be at war with people in your own community. You can be at war with your family. And, in many cases you can be at war with other businesses. This is all ego-driven. You will never be satisfied if you only listen to and pay attention to what the ego wants. The ego only wants to be separate. Only until you feel compassion for others will you understand what living is truly about. You can never live a life of peace and continue to feel separate and dominant.

Exercise - Monitoring

You cannot change what you cannot acknowledge. Be continuously aware of your ego. Have you ever heard the expression, "Keep your ego in check"? This is good advice.

Continue to check up on your own ego. Whenever you notice yourself putting others down, blaming the system, trying to control everything or engaging in a fight for dominance, stop yourself and notice what you are doing.

This is a never-ending process. Do not get discouraged. You must constantly be aware of the ego's need to dominate. The first step is to simply notice that you are doing it. This is not always easy. You have years of programming that has taught you the need to dominate others. Therefore it may take several years of noticing that you are doing it in order to change. But again, you cannot change what you cannot notice.

Whenever my ego creeps up on me, I remember to say a particular phrase that has helped me calm the power of ego and keep it at bay. The phrase that I use is, "Thanks for sharing."

Try it for yourself. Whenever you feel the need to put others down or dominate them, say that phrase to yourself, over and over again. "Thanks for sharing." You cannot fix a problem with the same mind that created it. The mind that created your problems is ego driven. Only when you step back from your ego can you begin to see the true egoic mind. Be aware and ever diligent in witnessing your egoic mind in action.

Chapter 2—The Fear of Money

During those early years, money was always tight. So, I always had a job. Of course, Brantford was a working town, and so everybody worked. I wasn't afraid of work: If I wanted something, I knew I had to pay for it somehow. I didn't really like my job and most certainly would have preferred doing something else, but like with most people, it was a means to an end. My mentality was that, in order to make money, I had to work hard.

I had several jobs. I started with a paper route, worked as a pizza delivery boy, labored five years as a landscaper, played the piano part-time in a pizza restaurant in between delivering pizzas, worked for my father part-time in his small moving company, fixed up and restored rusted cars and I did all of this before the age of 16.

Then, between 16 and 17, I worked on the assembly line building school buses for Bluebird International. I did this for two summers in my final years of high school. Then, right out of high school, I got a job working for a company called Malcolm Condensing. Now, that was one tough gig! They made powdered milk and powdered cheese for various products like Doritos. Have you ever scraped dried milk off of walls in 100° heat? As you can imagine, that was stomach curdling and not very fun at all. For nine bucks an hour, I can't imagine anything much worse. However, I caught a lucky break, tearing up my knee on the job. You're probably thinking to yourself, "how can a torn knee be lucky?" Simple: It was my ticket out of there.

My full-time employment salary was covered under something called the Workmen's Compensation plan. It started paying me about 80 percent of my wages without me having to work. I took the money and went back to school.

The only thing I really knew how to do (outside of manual labor) was play music. With that in mind, I applied for and was accepted to the Mohawk College of Applied Arts. To be specific, the jazz program. I really didn't know what else to do with my life, and it seemed like a good idea at the time. Maybe I could become a professional musician? Maybe I could end up teaching music? Whatever was to become of this choice, at least it was anything but working my butt off in a dead-end factory job—not that I have anything against people who work day-in and day-out in factory jobs. In fact, I truly appreciate and am grateful for those who do this so that I don't have to.

This was a very enjoyable period in my life. Mohawk College was the closest college to me as I was still living at home in Brantford. I learned a lot about music there, and I also learned a lot about relationships. I made the trek every day to Hamilton. It was good to get out of Brantford for the first time and spread my wings.

There were many great musicians at this college. This crushed my young ego. I did not know at the time that this was my ego's way of separating itself from others. My relationships were shallow and non-fulfilling. I did not know what it meant to support other people. I only wanted to be better than them. Do you ever feel like the only way to feel self-worth is to best others? It's not exactly the best path to making friends.

After three years of Mohawk College music training, I still wasn't that great of a musician. I decided to apply to another university to get even better at performing and in case I needed a piece of paper to say that I could teach. That way, I'd have something to fall back on. The University of Concordia in Montréal, Quebec, accepted me.

By this time, money was scarce. Working while attending full-time college studies was just not sustainable. I applied for student loans and packed up everything that could fit into my beat-up Chrysler station wagon. With a final glance in my review mirror, I headed off to a new life in Montréal.

University seemed like a really good choice at the time. But, looking back, I can honestly ask, "What was I thinking?"

It's not that university wasn't fun or that I didn't learn anything. I did. But, the problem I began to realize with the University school system was that I could only learn from the people around me, and all the professors teaching at that time had the same teaching method: lecture, lecture, lecture. What's more, none of them were professional musicians! Can you see the problem with wanting to be a professional musician by learning from people who are not?

I'm not saying that they were not good teachers. However, people often refer to certain teachers they had who became powerful mentors. I never had that relationship with any of my teachers there.

In my third year of university, I still didn't have enough credits to graduate, but there were simply not anymore courses that drew my interest. Thankfully, I had the opportunity to make up what is called a *self-directed elective*. I had to make up my own curriculum and have it approved and overseen by one of the music professors. The curriculum that I made up was to compose and arrange five complete pieces for big band, which included 17 musicians: trumpets, saxophone, rhythm section, piano, and bass. Anyone who knows anything about composition could tell you that I wasn't making it easy for myself: this was lot of work.

I was supposed to see the professor throughout the year, but I didn't see him at all, as he didn't have time. However, he did manage to sit down with me for one hour at the end of the year.

He skimmed his way through the charts, gave me an "A" and said, "Thank you very much."

And, that was it.

I asked," will there be an opportunity to hear this music that I've written? Is it possible to get played in the next big band rehearsal?"

" Not really," he said." We don't really have time for that."

And that was that. All he did was circle some of the mistakes, made a few brief suggestions, and sent me on my way—all that work for less than one hour of insufficient feedback.

I wondered, "What does this have to do with the artistic process?"

Then, it suddenly dawned on me—my professor, nor any professor who had taught me, really cared! And, to make matters worse, none of them were professional musicians!"

Throughout University I lived by myself in a tiny apartment on the 12th floor of a high-rise. It was a single-room apartment and the rent was $420 month. My entire budget for the month was $450, and so financially, things were pretty tight.

However, my biggest problem at that time was not the fact that I didn't have a lot of money, but the fact that I didn't have many friends. At that time anyone who was French-speaking from Québec could get his or her entire tuition paid for by the Québec government to study in English. Largely because of this incentive, most of the student body in the music department was actually French-speaking. Even though the language of instruction in the classroom was English, everyone spoke French outside the classroom. This made it very difficult for me to make friends, since, other than learning a little bit of it in high school, I really didn't understand anything that they were saying.

I felt alone. I also realized that, if I didn't learn to speak French quickly, then I would likely never have any friends from that school at all. So, I enrolled in a French course at the University and started watching French television.

Once I made the effort to speak a little French, I started meeting some really cool people. There was Francois Glazer, a guitar player who became a good friend and helped me out with my French during band practice. I ended up playing in a wedding band with him and a few other guys to make some extra money.

My personal piano teacher at this time was a very eccentric little man named Art Roberts. Mr. Roberts lived in a tiny little house in an area that can only be described as the wrong side of the tracks.

And lucky me had to take the Metro to his place every week for my piano lesson. Part of my university tuition included these private lessons. And, as eccentric and quirky as he was, he was the best jazz master I had met to date.

The epitome of the quintessential jazz guy, he had gray hair, stood about 5' 5" tall, made few friends, and—like many jazz musicians—chain-smoked both cigarettes and the other stuff. Every week we would go down to his tiny basement, which looked like a 1950s strip club, and he would lay on me some pretty cool lessons. He was a good teacher.

One of the coolest things he did was transcribe solos from a famous jazz bebop saxophone player named Sonny Stitt. Then, he pulled out of those solos short phrases, which he called "Stitt's Bits." He would give these to me as jazz patterns to study and learn by heart.

It was a marvelous way of teaching piano and one of the few ways that actually helped me learn. Being able to break things down to the lowest common denominator and learn from the ground up was an invaluable skill. I learned jazz like this, for the most part. I remember being so happy that I finally had some structure, and, without question, he helped advance my playing.

But (literally) poor Art did nothing to advance my mindset as a professional musician or help me move beyond poverty-stricken thinking. Sure, he was a good piano player, but he really couldn't help me become successful because he didn't know how to get past being poor. I should have taken note of this at the time, but I didn't.

I should have thought to myself, "Hey, is this where I am going to end up, teaching students in a dingy basement?" No offense to Art, but that was not the life for me.

My financial situation continued to get worse. I applied for more student loans, worked gigs on the side, and eventually started wrangling in some serious gigs in downtown Montréal. All musicians who aspire to be professionals eventually find themselves on the bandstand. I auditioned for a spot in a show band and got the gig.

The leader of that band was the worst trumpet player of all time. However, he was good at getting gigs, and so we worked a lot.

I should've realized at the time that this band really wasn't all that successful beyond getting a lot of gigs. But, again, I didn't care about all that. All I wanted to be was an artist. I got paid anywhere from $75 to $150 a night, and for me that was good money. It was never enough, but at least it kept me going.

The concept that money is hard to come by was what I grew up with. It was all I knew. All through University I struggled with money. Day after day I would find evidence to prove how hard it was to make money. Looking back, I wonder how things might have been different if I knew then what I know now. Of course, how could I have known what I know now? Many of the things that I learned about poverty, I learned through those trying times. It was also those times that have made me truly appreciative of what I have today.

Lesson— Becoming an Excellent Money Manager

One of the first things that you will have to come to terms with if you are ever to see any real money or wealth in your life is the concept of becoming a good *money manager.*

Most people avoid dealing with money. Why? Because *money is a source of pain for most people.* Let me rephrase that. The *lack of money* is a source of pain for most people.

Poverty is not having no money. It is a mindset. It is so powerful a reality changer that many people believe it is more righteous to be poor.

If you think about it, managing your money requires you to focus on how it comes in and how it goes out, and how you save it and how you invest it. However, if there is always a shortage of money, you will feel a tendency to want to avoid this task. Money tends to be a painful thing because who wants to manage something that isn't there? It can be embarrassing. Because most people suffer from lack, which is the fear that there's never enough, they simply put the thought of managing money on the back burner and forget about it.

Forgetting about money because you're feeling that there will never be enough will bring exactly what you focus on. The thought that there is never enough will bring more of the exact scenario: not enough, never enough.

I will discuss the Law of Attraction in detail later in this book, but, for now, simply recognize one thing: avoiding money is not a plan. Hoping that money will come in at the same time that you are avoiding it is ludicrous. You can only get what you focus on and what you pay attention to.

Learning to be a good money manager will require you to learn how to deal with money. You will need to learn how to make more or earn more. You will also need to learn what to do with it when it comes tumbling in. If you hoard it or stockpile it, then you will cut off the flow of money. How, you ask, does that work? In laymen terms, your fear of never having enough will bring your fears—that object of your focus—into reality.

Pay attention to your finances. They will not go away on their own, and they will certainly not right themselves on their own. Good money behaviors and good money habits are learned behaviors. Take a good, hard look at where you are financially, and where you want to get.

Chapter 3 - University

During my second year of university, things seemed like they were going pretty well: I was keeping up with my studies and practicing piano a fair amount. I was always busy and I felt productive.

However, I wasn't eating very well. I couldn't afford to eat more than a meal a day and so I would distract myself by playing piano or studying. Of course, one day it all caught up with me and I ended up in the hospital due to malnutrition. Apparently you cannot survive on cheap hot dogs and pita bread. It was then that I realized that maybe I couldn't look after myself as well as I thought. So I did what any self-respecting, yet somewhat confused and overwhelmed young man would do—I got married.

It's funny where things lead. A few years earlier, during my summers in high school, my brother and I took up waterskiing. We worked hard, played hard, and lived for the weekends on the water. That was our thing. In fact it's still my thing today. This past winter a friend of mine and my son went to the Toronto Boat Show and we all went indoor wake boarding. What a blast!

Anyway, during my summers waterskiing as a teenager, I had met a girl. Her name was Barbara and she came from a fairly stable and respected working-class family. And while I don't remember spending much time with her or even going on a date, I do remember that she had expressed interest in seeing me. I had lost track of her during my initial year and a half at University but after my bout with malnutrition somehow, as fate would have it, we agreed to meet at Christmas time at my parent's house in Brantford Ontario.

I really didn't know what to expect and, quite frankly, didn't give it much thought. But when she showed up one evening for dinner, I noticed that she wore tight-fitting jeans and had long flowing blonde hair, and I was surprised that such a beautiful girl aimed her attention squarely at me for the entire night. I thought to myself, "Okay, well, this is cool."

After going back to school in Montréal for semester two, we stayed in touch by phone. Things became serious between us and, little by little, as these things do, it progressed to the point where we began to discuss marriage. I saw this marriage as not just a romantic adventure but also an opportunity to work together as a couple to tackle financial challenges and University challenges.

Next thing I know, we're engaged to be married and set a date for the summer. I drove back and forth a few times from Montréal to southern Ontario to be with her, but each time I did I became less and less infatuated, and the initial spark of our relationship seemed to dull. However, when one makes a commitment to marry—let me rephrase that—when I make a commitment to marry, I take it seriously. However, even though my level of commitment is high, three days before our actual wedding day, I called my father from Montréal and told him that I wasn't going to go through with it. I tried to make a case that I wasn't ready and felt like I was being forced into it. He wasn't buying it, however, because he and many other people had spent many hours and a lot of money planning that wedding. He basically told me, "Get yourself to this wedding or else."

I guess there really wasn't much I could say to that and so the next day I got in my car and drove the seven hours to my parents house and spent the next two days preparing myself mentally for marriage.

I eventually came around to the thought that it wouldn't be that bad. She was a nice girl and quite beautiful. I'm sure I could find a way to make it work. Even though it wasn't 100 percent planted in my mind that this was going to turn out perfect, I tried to visualize marriage the way it's supposed to be. Whatever that is.

One of the things that I thought about was the concept of teamwork and how much easier University would be if she could work and bring in some money while I studied. As a college-trained dental technician it would be pretty easy for her to get a job, which for me meant not having to work so hard while I went to school. Right after we got married we moved in together in Montréal, and she quickly got a job as a dental assistant on the West Island. As the major breadwinner, every morning she would get up early and board the train for her one-hour trip to a dental office on the West Island. She couldn't speak French and never learned, but on the West Island this wasn't necessary, as the vast majority of their patients were English and the rest of the staff could speak French.

It all happened so fast. Before I knew it I was living a married life.

Even during our very first year together, I started to feel very strongly that we had made a mistake. We were two completely different people with two completely different career ideas that took us in two very different directions. If you think about it, what does a dental technician and a jazz musician have in common? The answer is not much.

However, I was raised to be loyal and faithful and so I did my best, at least in my mind, to make the relationship work. I was as attentive as I could be, but I could tell that she was not happy with my overall behavior or my aloofness. Call it intuition, call it whatever you like, but I knew that she knew that I was not completely committed to the relationship.

Then, in our second year together, in an effort to fix our seriously flawed relationship, Barbara got pregnant and I became an overnight father. What were we thinking bringing a child into our relationship? Anyway, Danielle was born and there really wasn't much I could do about that. She was a beautiful child and I loved her. Because my wife Barbara went to work every day, and money was short, I spent much of the first two years of Danielle's life raising her and looking after—at least during the day.

Through it all, even though I did my best as a father and I got by as a husband, I could feel the walls of responsibility welling up around me, literally choking me. I was an artist at heart and all Barbara wanted was stability. There is no such thing as a stable life as a jazz musician. She was constantly telling me to settle down and get a good job. She truly wanted me to be normal and like everyone else who worked for a living. I didn't mind working for a living; I had worked hard all of my life. Yet, music was now my sole career choice. And while she didn't see it as real work because of its instability, I did. Music was the only thing that I had ever loved, so I saw no reason to change my course—no matter how much she or anyone else wanted me to.

To deal with the anxiety of marriage and the stresses of fatherhood, I began working as much as I could. I went out into the world and took as many playing gigs as I could: I played piano in bars, hotels, weddings, bar mitzvahs—anything and everything. Then one day I landed a very nice, stable piano gig at the Delta hotel in downtown Montreal. It lasted three years and it paid pretty well. And, even though I didn't need the extra money, I still took many other gigs on top of that just to keep from going home.

Responsibility kept pressing in on me and I couldn't shake it. But, just when I thought it couldn't get any worse, I was sucked into suburban hell when Barbara and I decided to buy a semi-detached piece of property closer to her work on the West Island in Pointe Claire. This meant that I had to commute to downtown Montréal, but luckily, it also meant more time away from home.

After looking after my daughter Danielle all day, I would leave at 4 pm, get downtown by 5, play at the Delta hotel from 5 – 8 pm and then walk a few blocks down the street to Hotel de la Montagne and play another jazz gig from 10 until 2 in the morning. Ah, Hotel de la Montagne, now that was a great gig.

It was a fantastic jazz gig where I could stretch my musical muscle and dive into the intricacies of jazz with some great musicians. That gig taught me a lot about music, as night after night we would play some amazing renditions of popular jazz standards and even some popular funk music. I have fond memories of the hotel and all of the music played there.

Of course, my wife Barbara had very little to do with this environment. It was downtown and she was on the West Island—two worlds that never meet. With me working every night and my wife working all day, it was a constant source of conflict. It took just under three years for us to grow completely apart.

During those three years I moved into a separate bedroom in the basement because I literally could not handle the conflict between us. The constant talk about security and a better job was like hearing fingernails on a chalkboard to my still-young ears. Her constant mantra of "be secure, get a good job, work hard" was so boring to me. It so rubbed me the wrong way, over and over.

Yet, no matter what anyone thinks, I feel in my heart that I truly hung in there as long as I could for my daughter Danielle. I'm sure that one day she will pick up this book and read it.

"Danielle, if you are reading this, you need to know that I did my best. You were not at all the cause of my marriage problems. It was a disaster of our own making. I was miserable and angry all the time and, no matter how much I tried, I could not shake the weight, the pressure, and the responsibility. I truly feel that if we had stayed together for your sake, you would not be the kind, compassionate and loving soul that you are today. I'm sorry, please forgive me, I love you, thank you."[2]

I couldn't take it anymore. Our relationship had become a staring contest—both of us knowing it was making each of us unhappy, both of us just as stubborn to stick it out. Well, I lost the staring contest. One day in a final grand gesture of frustration, anger and even contempt, during a weekday when Barbara was at work, I rented a small moving truck, backed it up to the front door and I took my piano, a bed, a desk, and most of my clothes and moved out. I moved into a small, shared apartment in downtown Montreal. I'm not proud of it and never will be. Perhaps one day Barbara will forgive me, but ultimately that's up to her. As evidenced by her aforementioned need for security, she immediately moved back home to Ontario and proceeded to marry one of her high school acquaintances who had a steady job. She got what she wanted and I wish her well on her journey.

---

[2] **Ho'oponopono** (ho-o-pono-pono) is an ancient Hawaiian practice of reconciliation and forgiveness. The main ho'oponopono cleaning tool is the mantra; "I love you, I'm sorry, please forgive me, thank you." By saying this over and over you are clearing the data or memories in your mind. If you are having a problem, such as a relationship problem, say to yourself, "I accept responsibility for my part in the relationship. There is something inside me causing this problem. I am sorry, I love you, please forgive me and thank you." Repeat this over and over to clear whatever memories or feelings you have about the relationship.

Where did that leave me? Well, even though I still didn't know exactly what I wanted for myself, I got out of a situation that I definitely did not want. I felt better after having made the decision to leave. The next few years would lay the framework for a committed life (or so I thought) as a professional musician.

Lesson - Spiritual Partnership

I have learned since my rocky marriage and eventual breakup with Barbara that you cannot fix a relationship with the same mindset that created it. My mindset was focused on anything but the relationship. I sought refuge in music and in a working life as a musician. When the other party in your relationship is seeking the security and comfort that comes from a steady income, it becomes nearly impossible to fix that relationship. If each mind in the relationship is set on what it wants and neither is willing to shift, you're going to have a bad time.

In the many years since those early days of marriage, I have come to the realization that many women, not just Barbara, are not seeking security but safety—the safety that comes from a husband. There is a big difference between security and feeling safe. One can only feel safe when the people around them make them feel that way. I of course did not do this. How could I make her safe when I was never home? How could I make her feel safe when I did not support her in her life and work?

In addition to feeling safe, women also want to feel valuable and loved. There is nothing quite as powerful as a husband saying "Thank you" to a wife for the many things she does. When I look back, I do want to thank Barbara for those years she gave to me. I'm grateful.

Feeling loved is another thing entirely. A wife truly wants to feel loved, not just by what the husband says but also by what he does. Feeling loved is a state of being. It is a state of feeling like someone else is truly emotionally connected with you. It is more than just a physical sensation: it is a spiritual connection.

I'm not playing favorites here. Of course, these rules and laws also apply to men. Men also want to feel safe, valuable, and loved. However, my personal experience tells me that women seem to need it more, or in a different manner than men.

When was the last time you made the partner in your life feel safe, valuable, and loved? If you truly want to have a powerful relationship, then you will have to shift your mindset in that direction and behave differently. Make your actions proof of your intention.

Gary Zukav[3], a well-known spiritual leader, talks about the concept of *spiritual partnership*. I am in complete agreement with this concept. A spiritual partnership is defined as a partnership amongst equals for the purposes of spiritual growth. Essentially what that means is that you have a duty and responsibility to help and guide your partner to a life that is spiritually connected to their desires. You must go beyond selfishness and dedicate a portion of your life to nurture the needs and desires of your spiritual partner. You must praise them as well as love them. You must be in gratitude for them as well as challenge them to greater heights. A spiritual partnership is a team dedicated to a singular goal. If your goals do not match, then you do not have a true spiritual partnership.

---

[3] Gary Zukav, Spiritual Partnership: The Journey to Authentic Power

Your most powerful relationships will not come from power over others but from giving, caring, and nurturing. You were put on this earth not to take from others but to help them. Your best relationships require deep commitments to others before yourself. If it is support that you want then, you must first give the very thing that you are looking to get. You must offer your support and unconditional guidance to a spiritual partner before you can receive anything in return. This is a natural law of the universe; what you give out you will get back. There is an equal and opposite for everything in the universe. For every giver you need a receiver. Practice giving to your spiritual partner and then learn to be a grateful receiver.

Chapter 4 - A Yahoo! Moment

Near the end of my marriage to Barbara and during the first few months of my time in the shared apartment in downtown Montréal, I continued playing jazz four nights a week at Hotel de la Montagne. The words that I would choose to describe this hotel are *Italian bordello*. It was truly a sight to see, with over-the-top ornate sculptures, marvelous fountains, and rococo architecture. It was popular with the wealthier, career-minded go-getters of Montréal—many who were single. Some of them were looking for playmates, and some of them were looking for marriage.

It just so happens that I made friends with one of the ones who were looking for marriage. He was a very successful self-made high-level salesperson for a huge IT company called Oracle. He wasn't super rich, but nobody would ever call him broke. His name was Robert (Rob) Roy, a French Canadian who spoke perfect English. He started frequenting the piano bar as a jazz lover and we hit it off. He began to come to the club pretty much every night. Yes, he really enjoyed the music, but he also had an ulterior motive. He was looking for a girlfriend and maybe even a wife. And, because the piano attracted women like moths to a flame, it was the perfect place for him to hang out.

There always seem to be a plethora of women to talk to, and Rob did his best to meet as many of them as he could. He also relied on me to break the ice, as it was my territory. It was a mutually beneficial relationship: I was a starving artist who could attract the women and he was wealthy enough to pay for dinner.

One night Rob came into the bar and sat at the bar stool closest to me. He seemed unusually excited.

"What's up?" I asked him curiously.

"Take a break. I need to talk to you about something." I couldn't tell if he was excited or agitated.

"I'm playing right now; can't it wait? I can't just take a break whenever I want to," I replied.

"Okay, but as soon as you can take a break, I've really got something important to tell you."

After three or four rather lengthy jazz songs, Rob was looking increasingly impatient. I couldn't take the suspense any longer, either, and so I ended the set early, walked over to the bar, grabbed my usual rusty nail with ice and joined Rob at the piano bar. "Okay, what's so important that you needed to interrupt my set? "

He started in, "Have you ever heard of a company called Yahoo!?"

"Yahoo? Isn't that something they yell at a hockey game when somebody scores a goal?" I replied flippantly.

He explained, "No, it's a company that is going to help people find things on the internet."

I asked something that, at that time, was forgivable.

"What's the Internet?"

I don't really know if he thought I was kidding or not, but I didn't want to look stupid and I don't think he wanted me to look stupid either. So, he proceeded to tell me that Yahoo would be a major force on the Internet by helping people navigate the millions of terabytes of information that would eventually make up the World Wide Web.

"It's called a 'search engine", he explained, "Because it helps people find what they are looking for based on keyword searches."

I can't truly remember if I grasped the idea completely, but I was starting to see that this might be important stuff. To my own defense, you have to take into consideration that this was the year 1994, at the very infancy of the Internet, and I was an artist who didn't really know much of anything that was happening in the real world. I was by all accounts living underground. I didn't read the news (I couldn't afford to buy a newspaper), I paid child support, and I lived day-to-day.

"What does Yahoo! have to do with me anyway?" I asked.

He leaned in close and in a calm but convincing voice he said, "I want you to buy shares in Yahoo! and Invest in the company"

I wasn't sure what he meant by that. "You want me to buy shares? You mean like stock?"

He nodded.

"Dude," I responded, "does it look to you like I have any money to invest in anything? I could maybe sell my piano, and perhaps even my beat-up car to get a couple thousand bucks, but that's it. Then how would I get to my gigs and how would I practice the piano?"

He looked sincerely disappointed.

"Are you investing in it?" I asked.

"Of course. Paul, I'm in the IT business and when I tell you this thing's going to be big, it's going to be big!"

I kind of half-smiled at him to reassure him that, despite my not willing to invest, I was thankful for the information. While he seemed disappointed I could tell that he knew I was not only strapped for cash but also stuck in the mindset of someone who was not quite willing to take a risk.

Rob, of course, did invest in Yahoo! and a few years later I received an invitation to visit him and his new wife in their new Vermont home. I can remember very clearly taking that trip and winding up at the iron gates, which stood at the entrance to a half-mile driveway. As I proceeded down the driveway to his house, I realized that it was more than your average home. To me it seemed like a castle. It was situated a few hundred yards from the northern shore of Lake Champlain in upper state Vermont. What a view! There were a few luxury cars in the driveway and in the three-car detached garage. And when Rob came out of the house to greet me, I immediately asked the obvious question, "Where did all this come from?"

He simply replied with a big smile on his face, threw both of his arms in the air and shouted, "Yahoo!"

I certainly wasn't smiling quite as much as he was, but I commented sheepishly, "Rob, why didn't you coax me into buying stock if you knew for sure? You had your ear to the ground in terms of technology and you knew what was happening."

His response to that question is something I'll always remember, even though at the time it certainly wasn't what I wanted to hear.

"We all make choices in life," He said. "I guess you didn't really have a choice at that time. In your mind you simply didn't have the money and therefore you had no choice."

That's so true. One of the things I know today that I didn't really understand then is that money gives you more choices.

I knew he was trying not to force the issue or to make me feel bad about not having money, but, like I said, in my mind I hadn't had a choice. I likely could have come up with some money. Even if I invested the mere couple thousand dollars that my car and the piano would have brought me, I would have made some serious money—that stock went from under $2 a share to over $250 a share! I never knew exactly at what point Rob sold his stock, but I do know that he made a fortune. That was my first real initiation to the world of money.

Whatever jealousy I felt at that time is gone now, but I can tell you that I didn't feel at all happy about it. Perhaps it was at that moment that I first began the process of breaking down my prejudices and my feelings towards money. I mean, I could see what it could buy, and I was not at all disagreeable to the thought of that being me one day.

I remember feeling inadequate. My girlfriend, who had accompanied me during my visit Rob, assured me, as we lied on the comfortable beds in one of Rob's guest bedrooms, that I had nothing to feel inadequate about. My relationship with her was serious at the time, and we both agreed that we would do our best and that, for richer or for poorer, we would respectfully remember to take some risks.

The next day as we were leaving, I told Rob half-jokingly, "Listen Rob, when my Yahoo! moment comes back again, I'm in."

While my Yahoo! moment never came as a result of Rob Roy, it did come several years later. I guess one never truly knows when a Yahoo! moment comes along. I learned to keep my eyes open and seek out opportunities rather than have them come to me.

Lesson—Why take a risk?

Most people like to play it safe. Let me rephrase that: Most people *only* play it safe. There are a number of reasons for this, not the least of which is the concept that somehow you are more secure if you don't take risks. However, in my experience the only risk in life is *not* taking one.

When you take no risks, nothing changes, and you learn nothing. One of the most powerful concepts that Suggestology teaches you is that; when you take an action, whether risky or not, you always learn *something*.

The last thing I would want to happen in my life is to look back and realize that I played it safe. Where is the fun in that anyway? I want to look back and be proud of the risks that I took and the mistakes that I made and the successes that I achieved. Naturally, for most people, the concept of failure is very scary. However, for me, failure is a natural progression on the way to achieving desires.

In order to achieve something you may have to fail many times. Thomas Edison said, "Success is 99 percent failure." And, while that may be true, in my experience you don't need to fail that much in order to get where you're going.

Making corrections along the way is a natural part of Suggestology and the learning process. However, you cannot learn anything if you are so afraid of failure that you never start anything or risk anything.

If comfort is your disease of choice and you are truly averse to risk then you would do well to read the following story about you:

Picture yourself with both hands grasping strongly to a trapeze bar while swinging back and forth high above the ground. You are swinging back and forth at a medium pace. It is a fairly comfortable activity for you, and your arms and hands are strong enough to hold you. As you look down you recognize that the ground is moving beneath you and you continue to swing back and forth.

Now picture this swinging motion as the same motion that you use to swing through life. You work all week feeling like you're swinging backwards because the very thought of going to work is something that you have to do and not something that you want to do. Then you swing forward a little bit on the weekend as you enjoy the things that you like to do. Then when Sunday night comes, you begin to swing backward again into the thought of going back to work.

Once in a while you swing forward because an activity comes into your life that you enjoy doing, such as golfing or horseback riding. But eventually you have to swing backward because that thought of security takes over and you have to get back to work. You may not like it, but you are comfortable in this life as you swing backwards and forwards.

You have some ups and you have some downs; you face some challenges and you overcome some obstacles. But nothing really changes. Your circle of influence has not changed. You are not any wealthier now than you were 10 years ago. Your relationships have not changed much. And essentially, you struggle through life wondering when things will change, wondering when things will get better. But they won't. You're just swinging a little bit ahead, and with every swing forward there is an inevitable swing backward.

Then one day someone comes to you with an opportunity. As you dangle from your trapeze bar, you look ahead and see that someone is hanging upside down on an opposite trapeze bar. Every time you swing forward, they are there within 10 feet from you. As you swing backward, they also swing away from you. Every time you meet and get close, you realize that this is the opportunity that you have been waiting for. Yet, because they are still no closer than 10 feet away, it represents a tremendous amount of risk for you to let go, jump and experience the opportunity.

Eventually, the opportunity that existed, which is the person who was there willing to catch you, has moved on. You are left by yourself, swinging back and forth.

Then another day, another opportunity in the form of someone else on the opposite trapeze bar swings towards you. This time, they look stronger and it feels safer. And all of a sudden, you decide to jump. You don't try anything too difficult because this is the first time you are taking the risk. You throw your legs towards the other person and you keep your eye on them and pray for dear life.

Just as you begin to turn upside down, and feel as if you have perhaps made a horrible mistake, you feel hands around your ankles. They catch your legs. You breathe a sigh of relief. And it feels good to have taken the risk because now you have a different perspective. You are not only just swinging back and forth, you're swinging back and forth with another person, and your perspective has changed because you are viewing the ground from a different angle.

What did you learn? You learned that the world looks different. You learned that sometimes it's good to take a risk because change is exciting. You learned that you are not alone in your risk and that someone is there to catch you. You learned, in essence, to trust the process.

But now you are swinging back and forth upside down, and you realize that someone else is partly in control of your destiny. What now?

So you ask the person who's grasping you by the legs what to do. And they respond by telling you, "I can't hold on to you all day. You're going to have to leap back to the other trapeze bar. I can throw you and guide you as best I can, but I can't be there to catch you. You will have to do that on your own."

This is a scary thought—having to grasp the other trapeze bar on your own without anyone to catch you. What if the other bar doesn't get close and you fall? What if you're not strong enough to catch yourself? You're not used to jumping and grabbing on; you are only used to swinging back and forth.

But you have no choice. Because you took the initial risk, a new one has replaced it. You are now obligated to take the risk because the person that is holding you is getting tired. And the only way that they can revive their strength or be replaced by someone else is for you to let go and jump back to your original trapeze bar.

So you jump with all your strength and hope for the best.

But you miss. You begin the fall. And now you're scared. Really scared. Terrified. But somehow, even though you didn't notice it before, there has always been a net, it was just too far away and too out of focus for you to notice. Yet, there it is, and you fall directly into it. You are safe and grateful.

The net, by the way, is what is known as source energy, the universe, God, the creator, master of all things living. It is always there and always willing to catch those who are willing to jump. You did not know this before, but, because you took the initial risk, you now know that there is a net. You're not sure that it will always be there, but it was this time and maybe it'll be there next time.

So, you climb up the ladder, get back on your trapeze and start swinging again back and forth. This time things are different. Because you have experienced the concept of a universal net and you know that opportunity will appear sometime soon, you are anxious to get going. Because you are anxious and enthusiastic, all of a sudden the opportunity appears. This time it's someone different. They look different and smile differently, but they still represent a leap that you can take.

You think to yourself, I can jump the same way as last time, but what will I learn? I want to learn something new. It felt good the last time I learned something so how can I learn something new this time? You think to yourself, What if this time I do a somersault? Maybe I'm not ready to do two somersaults just yet because I don't have that much practice, but what if I try just one? It's a little riskier than the first time that's for sure.

Then you remember the net—a universal net that will be there to catch you. And even before you realize it, are letting go, and before you have time to be frightened, you are tumbling through the air. This time as you tumble, you are learning to fly. And just as you get comfortable with flying, you are caught. You have reached your destination and achieved your goal. It feels good but not good enough. Why? Because you could have done two somersaults instead of one. You could have learned to fly differently. So you quickly jump back to the other trapeze bar and keep a lookout for the next opportunity to do a double, triple, and maybe a quadruple somersault with a triple twist. Each and every time you raise the bar on what you are able to do. You do this because it feels good. Because it feels right. Because it is what you are up there to do. What else could you be up there for?

And as you somersault through the air learning to fly, you recognize once and for all that the only true way to live your life to the greatest possible extent that you can live is to learn how to fly with ease, agility, grace, and difficulty all at the same time.

Once in a while, yes, you fall. But somehow the universal net is always there. And because now you have likely fallen many times, you are feeling invincible.

Eventually you look back at your life that you lived swinging back and forth, never risking and always playing it safe and you consider:

If I had only learned to fly sooner...

As we grow older, it's not the things we did that we often regret, but the things we didn't do. That's why we have tomorrows—for us to make things up.

You must understand that, if you are to achieve anything in life, you will have to take a risk. There simply is no other way. And if you are thinking to yourself that you have taken too many risks and failed to continue risk-taking, take a moment to reflect on what you have learned each and every time you fell. If you are unhappy with your results, you are likely following the same actions, resulting in the same mistakes over and over again. You are letting go of the trapeze, but not extending yourself to receive what's coming to you. But that's okay. Remember, it's only a mistake if you make it twice. You must build on your mistakes, as we all do. But if you are going to fail, fail forward.

Chapter 5—Limiting Beliefs

My dad, Arthur Tobey, is an ordained United Church minister. This meant that during the years that I was growing up, not only was he a servant of the church, but, as such, he was a very busy guy as you could imagine. Being a minister also meant that money was never a priority. Don't get me wrong—we weren't starving, but it always seemed to me that money was hard to come by. If you wanted something, my family's mindset was that you had to get it for yourself: You had to work for it and, more often than not, you had to work hard.

My dad worked hard. Because of the financial implications of the ministry, he had to start a one-truck moving business on the side just to get by. I worked as much as I could in that moving business carrying boxes and furniture up and down stairs all day. In hindsight I appreciate the quality time spent with my father during these jobs. Between the church and the moving business, after all, he really didn't have much time left over.

Around the time when I was in my early teens, my dad wrote a book called *I Believe*. The book was a collection of articles from a newspaper column, which he wrote for the local newspaper, the *Brantford Expositor*.

He was proud of the book and ordered a printing of several cases. But, like any author, he quickly realized that books don't just sell themselves. He was going to have to come up with a plan to sell his book. So, he decided that the next logical step was to open his own Christian bookstore. He borrowed $25,000 from the bank and opened a store right across the street from the church. Not knowing much about the bookstore business or retail business in general, he took on a partner who had a bit more business experience than he did. Sadly, it turned out that the experience this "partner" had was in being shady.

This partner of his was only in our lives for a very short time—just long enough to take the entire $25,000 and skip town. We never saw him after that. The cloud of darkness that descended on our family after that strangled out any hope or happiness we had been salvaging during an already rough period.

My mother seemed to get the worst of it. The loss of that money sent her into a victim tailspin. She cried at the dinner table almost every night. For two years. My brother Martin and I, oblivious to the crushing weight of her circumstance, used to make fun of her when she did that, calling it the "head-in-the-hand trick." She wouldn't eat at the table at all. She would just sit there and cry with her head propped up against her hand with her elbow on the table. It was so incredibly depressing to see her and my dad—and the entire family, for that matter—go through such a heart-wrenching experience. I wish I could go back in time and write that poor family a check for $25,000. It seems like such a small amount of money now. Of course, to them, at that time, losing it was the end of the world.

This was the beginning of my fear of money. When you experience the darkness and depression firsthand that a lack of money can manifest, you begin to associate money with pain.

When I thought of money, I thought of the following phrases:

"Money doesn't grow on trees."

"Money is hard to come by."

"Money is the root of all evil."

"You have to work hard to get ahead."

If I were to ask my dad for anything he would say something like, "What do you think I am, made of money?"

Do any of these phrases sound familiar to you?

My parents belief system became my belief system. You worked hard for your money. The lack of money was so stressing that mom would cry at the dinner table every night and so my dad would work even harder. As a result, I ended up spending less time with them. They probably thought I was fine, hanging out with friends or playing my music—doing kid things—but the fact is that today I don't really know my parents that well because I didn't get the chance. Maybe I didn't want to know them. Maybe, subconsciously, I didn't want to be near all that pain.

I tell people that I came from the "It'll do" family. We never had a new car because a used one—"It'll do." I never had nice new clothes because hand-me-downs—"They'll do." We rarely ate out at restaurants because a good home-cooked meal—"It'll do."

I remember being 13. Like most 13-year-olds, I wanted to fit in, and fitting in meant getting a pair of Levis like everyone else had. Instead, my mother bought me the stiffest pair of jeans that you could possibly get from Woolworths, a steal at $1.99. And that was a good day. Most of the time I would get my older brother's hand-me-downs.

My family bordered the poverty line. My mother shopped at three different stores on Saturdays just to get the best deals on groceries. I can't even imagine that way of life now, but back then it was my reality. And, as my parents believed, so did I.

Granted, this is of course my perception and my perception alone. In all fairness, life could have been something completely different to my parents during these times. I must say, however, that seeing my parents go through this period of scraping by in their lives was easily as painful for me as it was for them.

Lesson—Learning How to Get What You Want

What did I learn about money during my childhood from my parents, who worked hard but struggled to provide? Money equals pain. And, of course, as I thought about money and equated it with pain, I subconsciously avoided it. Why would I want something in my life that caused me pain? Because of this belief, I lived most of my life with next to nothing. I would work hard to earn it, but I never had more than just enough.

What did you learn from your parents? Are your perceptions and prejudices about money the same as mine were? Think about your upbringing and try to remember some of the things your parents would say or do surrounding the topic of money. Did they talk about money at all or did they keep that world hidden from you?

Despite my personal lessons that told me money equals pain, I still knew fundamentally that I also needed it to survive. Many people say that money is not important. Of course, they usually say this right until the point where they don't have any to spare. It's at that point that it becomes very important. Money was very important to me if I wanted or needed anything. So, I always worked hard to get it. Working hard was the only way I was taught to get anything. I have learned over the years, though, that working hard is only a small part of the equation. In fact, I no longer believe that you need to work hard to get ahead.

What is it that you need to do instead? It comes down to two things:

1. Learn from someone who has what you want, and

2. Make sure that others benefit from your actions.

I will discuss these elements in more detail throughout the book, but for now please understand two things: The first is that you cannot get what you want through trial and error alone. You have to learn from someone else—someone who has what you want and therefore possesses the roadmap to get where you want to go. The second is that the laws of giving are very clear; if you help others get what they want, then you will have what they have in abundance. This I am sure you have heard many times before in many different ways; what goes around comes around, what you give out you get back, as you sow so shall you reap. The universe always rewards you when you use your gifts to benefit others. However, what you may not know is that if you do not use your gifts for the benefit of others, the universe tends to take those gifts away from you—or at the very least it takes away your benefits from those gifts. All you really have to remember is this: If you're in it for yourself and you are the only one who benefits, then your success will be short-lived or in most cases *nonexistent.*

Suggestology can activate your natural will to learn. It is simply a matter of questioning everything that you know. In fact, for the most part it's not what you don't know that keeps you from success, but what you know that isn't necessarily so.

If you believe that money is hard come by then you will attract the very thing that you believe and find plenty of evidence to prove that you are right. This is an essential part of the success equation: to believe it is to see it.

Most people believe only in what they can see. And, of course, what they see proves that their beliefs are correct. The unfortunate part is that most people have limiting beliefs.

A *limiting belief* is a thought or perception, which is usually planted early on and nurtured by an environmental influence, that limits a person's ability to attain their goals. For example, your parents, teachers, friends, colleagues, and even the media around you are huge influencers in the formation of your belief system. However, what they believe or purport to believe may not be the actual truth. Just because they are older than you does not mean they have truer belief systems—indeed, many have become cemented over the years in very limiting beliefs. Because these influencers surround you during your formative years, you become infected with their limiting beliefs.

Only Suggestology can help you overcome these barriers, and it does that by forcing you to question your own belief systems and the belief systems of those who are close to you. Without questioning you cannot change. Without questioning you cannot grow. Without questioning you cannot possibly activate your natural learning process.

Think about it like this: If money is hard to come by then how come many people have a lot of money when most people don't? Is it simply the luck of the draw? No. The simple fact is; people that believe that money can flow easily into their lives have it flow easily. Those that worry about money, struggle with it and fear the fact that there will never be enough will attract the very thing that they focus on.

There has been much talk and mountains of literature in years regarding something called " the law of attraction." The law of attraction states that you attract whatever you give your energy, focus and attention to—whether you want to or not. In other words, what you focus on tends to be the very thing that you attract. Therefore, if you focus on not having enough you will not have enough and will never have more. Many people believe that the law of attraction is a made-up by a bunch of people who simply want to feel better about themselves. Nothing could be further from the truth. Actually, these people simply understand best that helping others reach their potential puts them in the perfect mind frame to attract their own wishes. In fact, everyone on planet Earth is a master of the law of attraction. However, most people do not realize it and therefore constantly attract into their lives the very things that they do not want. Your belief system magnetizes your level of attraction. If similar energies attract, then the energy you omit attracts the same frequency of energy.

Money is energy. It can flow easily and effortlessly in and out of your life, or you can interrupt its flow through a *lack mentality*. What is a lack mentality? It is a constant fear that there is never enough—that something will run out, that you can never save enough, that there is not enough to go around, that you cannot share because you do not have enough. What you really need to know is that lack mentality, worry, and fear are the enemy of success. And the more you lack, fear and worry, and the more you equate money with pain, the more money and abundance will be repelled from you. Until you understand and utilize the law of attraction to your benefit, you cannot possibly change your state of wealth. Have you ever thought about why it is that you are always short of money and feeling like you are one step away from total financial ruin?

Most people would rather be right about their own belief system then actually have what they want. It's more comfortable. Most people feel it is important to be right because it feels terrible when they're wrong. Therefore, when you always strive to be right, then you cannot be opened to new information and, as a result, are impervious to learning. The only way that you can begin to realize change is by counteracting that very belief system which you currently subscribe to by understanding how to ask yourself questions. Suggestology is the key to that change. You must ask yourself questions and be open to the answers.

The law of attraction simply responds to your focus. It does not seem to understand whether it is good for you or not. It just responds to energy. The energy that you put out, you will get back. If your belief system tells you that money is hard to come by, then you will constantly feel bad about the lack of money and continue to attract that negative state through the energy you use to focus on your lack of money.

Here is a simple Suggestology-based exercise that will get you started in asking yourself some deep and meaningful questions. They're designed to get you to realize that, until you come to terms with your limiting beliefs, there is no way for you to attract money.

I am going to help you identify your limiting beliefs. You cannot change what you cannot acknowledge, and so identifying your limiting beliefs is the first step—only then can you guide yourself towards change by learning to focus on the things that you do want instead of unintentionally focusing on the things that you do not.

It is important to know what you don't want in order to gain momentum towards the things that you do. However, this must be a brief exercise, because you want to start focusing on what you do want right away! Focusing on what you don't want makes it impossible for you to focus on what you do want. Try this: Don't think of a purple elephant with green spots on its ears and candy canes for tusks. Once you read that, it became impossible for you not to give your attention to it. In that way, it is important to remember that focusing on the things you do want is what will bring about positive and lasting change.

Exercise—Clear Out Limiting Beliefs

Draw a straight line down the middle of a piece of paper. On the top left-hand side, jot down the heading "Limiting Beliefs". On the right-hand side, put the heading "Empowering Beliefs".

On the left side, write down a list of all the things that you believe are holding you back. These are the things that you do not want but continue to attract into your life. Really dig deep. Cast a wide net.

When you're finished with that, on the right-hand side, write the corresponding positive and empowering message that will guide your subconscious into your new reality—that abundance is possible.

Here are some examples:

Limiting Beliefs (What you don't want.)	Empowering Beliefs
I never win anything.	People win prizes every day. I, too, am in the process of allowing prizes and other good things to happen to me.
I always struggle to pay the bills.	I have the ability to pay bills effortlessly and I am in the process of creating a steady cash flow.
I am horrible with money.	I am in the process of adopting good money behaviours.

I struggle to maintain my health.	I am committed to living a long and healthy life.

Please take the time to do this exercise right. Reading it in this book will do nothing for you—it is not enough to sit on the sidelines. You've tried that, we all have, and it doesn't do any good. Many people read things every day, but only experience matters. When you read something and form an opinion about it, you have learned little. Only when you participate in the exercises produced for your well-being can you gain the experience of what it means to attract into your life the things that you wish to attract.

To download a printable PDF worksheet of this exercise visit this url:

http://www.trainingbusinesspros.com/m /limiting-beliefs

So, did you do it yet?

Stop now and take the time to do the exercise. Exercises like this will activate your natural learning process through Suggestology and make you a lifelong learn-it-all, instead of a do-nothing know-it-all.

Chapter 6—Common Goals Teamwork

Teamwork and the utilization of strong team players is one of the hallmarks of successful people. It doesn't take a rocket scientist to figure out that, should you want to push a big boulder up a hill, having a big, strong group who are willing to help you will make everything go much easier and a heck of a lot faster.

Effective team players must share common goals. If you have one group trying to push the rock uphill while the other tries with all their might to push it down, not only is the boulder not going anywhere, but someone is probably going to get hurt. Because my first marriage to Barbara was in essence a defective team, based on the fact that neither of us wanted to end up at the same place, we were destined to failure. That relationship soured my perception of teamwork. It took several years for me to open up to the fact that a strong relationship could be powerful.

After the breakup of my marriage to Barbara, I threw myself completely into the business of music. This numbed the pain of failure.

It had been several years since our breakup and more than two years since the formal divorce. I was working in my second year as the leader of the house jazz band at Hotel de la Montagne in downtown Montréal. I had re-learned what it meant to be single. I was okay with where I was, I thought. Of course, what I unconsciously attracted was a whole different story.

It was a typical Saturday night, pretty much like every other Saturday. The bar was hopping, people were having fun chatting and listening to the jumping music which soared through the hall. However, there was one thing different on that fateful Saturday night. Unbeknownst to me at the time, a goddess had come to visit. To this day, I can remember the first time I laid eyes on her from across the smoky room as if it were happening in front of me now. The band and I were in the middle of a set of smokin' hot jazz when she, this beautiful blonde in a captivating red dress, cropped up into my vision.

My mind immediately began to wander from my music.

Of course, as the law of attraction states, you attract the very thing you focus on. The next thing I know, she's at the piano requesting a song from me. I'm pretty sure it wasn't me she was interested in but music that she could dance to, evidenced by the fact that she requested a Whitney Houston song even though we were playing jazz.

How could I refuse? I replied that, yes, I think I knew a couple of Whitney Houston songs, and if she'd just give me a moment to let my band mates know, we would perform it next.

So, right in the middle of a jazz set, we do this Whitney Houston song: "Saving All My Love For You." The next thing I know, everybody in the bar is dancing. This was certainly not normal. I can't even remember it happening one other time. Jazz musicians don't particularly like dancing because it distracts people from the overall purpose of the art behind the music. But I was captivated by her presence. And, as she danced with the manager of the bar, she never left my sight.

At my break, she sat down beside two other women. I did not know they were her sisters at the time. I boldly—okay, maybe a little less than boldly—walked up to her. See, I'm not usually shy when it comes to talking to women… but that doesn't mean I know what to say either. I said to her, "Hi, I'm Paul, the piano player guy."

She turned to me with a slightly confused look on her face. I could tell she didn't recognize me. But I was too deep to stop now. I said the first thing to I could think of, which was a testament to never saying the first thing that pops into your head:

"You don't really know anything about music, do you?"

Tilting her head, she looked at me funny and asked, "Who are you again?"

It didn't really bother me that she didn't remember me. To her I was just another nameless, faceless piano player. I did my best to make a graceful exit.

But disinterest is just a step or two away from adoration, right? It's at least not as far away as, say, disgust. A couple of weeks later, she showed up again, only this time with a friend. They both sat at the piano to my immediate right. On the break I talked to Nancy—the beautiful blonde—and her friend. I asked if she remembered me from two weeks ago. She said she did remember being there, but that she didn't remember me at all. Ouch. So why had she come back? It was her friend who had insisted on going there that night because, apparently, it was the friend who was interested in me.

I'm not quite sure how it happened, as things seemed to blur whenever I was around Nancy, but I ended up walking her friend to her car after the gig was over at about two in the morning. I, of course, had an ulterior motive in mind, which was to ask her for Nancy's phone number. It was clear that she did not want to give it to me, however, and was rather put off that I asked. In hindsight, it was a brash move. A brash move, I may add, that did not get me any phone numbers. But I knew what I wanted.

I remembered hearing of Nancy's work during the night, and, so—and this is a bit embarrassing to admit—I called her. At work. Does it relieve you to know that at least I knew how drawn I was to this woman? I called about three or four times, but the outcome wasn't good. Dating was obviously the furthest thing from her mind: It turns out that she had just come through a bitter breakup and was not interested at all in starting up with someone else.

So I gave up, right?

Hah! Now does that sound like me? No, I didn't give up—I got smart. I called her at around 4:30 on a Friday afternoon and made her an offer that I knew she couldn't refuse. I said, "I know you've been working really hard, and I know that you likely don't have any food in your fridge at home. Would you like to have supper with me, my treat?"

How I knew she didn't have any food in her fridge and why are still a mystery to her and me, I found out later that the only thing she had in her fridge was a lonely jar of mustard. At that time, I was living with a friend in a very upscale apartment at a renovated warehouse called the Candy Factory. My friend Eric was out of town on business and I had the entire place to myself.

"Here's the deal," I said. "I'll make you a nice dinner, and then I'll drive you home afterwards. I'll even make sure you're home by eight o'clock."

I was brash, but I drove a hard bargain. She agreed.

She came over and I made her a nice pasta dinner—gnocchi with some Alfredo sauce. Then afterward, I sat at my piano and asked what she'd like to hear. She requested a song by George Michael called "Careless Whisper." Thank God I knew that song. Perhaps you remember it. Here are some of the lyrics:

Time can never mend
The careless whispers of a good friend
To the heart and mind, ignorance is kind

There's no comfort in the truth, pain is all you'll find

I'm never gonna dance again
Guilty feet have got no rhythm...

I was about five minutes into the song and improvising on it when I turned around to see how she liked my impressive display. She was asleep. Well, I was true to my word. I woke her up at eight o'clock and told her that I needed to take her home. She said later that she was sad I took her home: She was comfortable and having a great time.

The next day I called her at the office and asked her to meet me afterword for coffee. In her words, the story goes something like this:

> *I was curious to hear from Paul again, but truth be told, I was not looking for a relationship. I was tired of men. So, he called me up and asked me to meet him at a coffee shop. I went home first and put on the ugliest set of clothes I could find just to turn him off.*

I remember those clothes, and I don't remember them looking ugly at all.

We kissed that night for the first time. Somehow, I knew that this relationship was special right away. And I knew that she knew it, too. In fact, just two weeks later, thieves ransacked her apartment and she was too scared to sleep there. She called me to see if she could come over to my apartment to spend the night.

She never left. We've been together ever since; 18 years at the time I'm writing this.

It was a strange relationship at the beginning, but fun. While she was just 23 at the time and I was 29, we had at times similar interests at others very different ones. For example, she was very focused on her job, friends, and parties, and I was, of course, immersed in music.

Money seemed very tight in those early days. I was paying all the bills. She was the one with the full-time corporate job, but somehow she never seemed to have any money, and that was something we did have in common. I was to learn that her belief systems about money were very similar to mine. The two of us attracted poverty.

Even after a year of seeing each other and living together, she was still going out with her friends on a regular basis and spending a lot of money on partying. I wanted to make sure that she was committed to the relationship.

After a year, I told her I thought it was time we found her a new place to live.

I was beginning to wake up to the importance of responsibility, of planning, and of looking to the future rather than burying my head in the work at hand. I had to know she was in it for the long haul and not just a free ride. She told me she was in it for good.

There are no instruction manuals to the perfect life. I was in blind territory: I had a woman who I loved very much, and I was learning how to be with someone again. It took me a while, but honestly, looking back, in your 20s, does anyone really know what they are doing? I will say that I was trying, I was learning, and I was discovering ... and that would make all the difference.

After several years of marriage to Nancy and living close to or slightly above the poverty line, I can tell you that I did not yet understand the concept of spiritual partnership. It was only at the point when we began to question our results did we begin to realize that, even as strong as our relationship was, it certainly didn't bring us closer to our goals. Nancy eventually gave up her corporate position and came into the music business as my personal manager. For the next several years, we struggled within the industry to find our way.

It has only been in the past few years that we have truly reached our stride. We did this by focusing on common goals. Only when we started discovering and implementing the art of Suggestology, by learning and questioning everything, did things begin to change for the better financially. And, funnily enough, as our finances improve our relationship gets stronger. Did you know that the number one cited cause of divorce amongst couples is a lack of money? Some may think that is the way it is because money is the most important thing in a marriage, but maybe being broke can be a symptom of a deeper problem—one of incongruity, of no focus—that can tear apart any relationship.

Where are you at in your relationships? Do the two of you share common goals and values? Do you question the way things are? Do you live life together, separate, or by default?

Exercise—True Heart's Desire

Sometimes, the smallest things can make the biggest difference. One of the things that truly helped my wife and I discover how we might work together better than we had before was to an exercise that I learned from the author, Dr. Robert Anthony. In his course entitled "The Secret Of Deliberate Creation", he discusses discovering what you want by asking yourself very important questions in a very specific way.

Again, I encourage you to do this exercise before moving on with this book. This exercise will activate your natural learning process and help you discover exactly what it is that you desire in this life. Isn't that worth your time? If you do it with your life partner, it can only serve to accelerate your success and strengthen your relationship.

Step #1

What do you want?

It seems like a simple question. But you need to answer this carefully. It's not about what you "think" you want, but about what you really want.

Have you ever heard the phrase "He has his heart set on something"?

Would you agree that "I'm thinking about getting that" is not as powerful as "My heart is set on getting that"? The energy is missing in the first one. The question you need to answer is, "What do I *really* want?" If there were no limitations, no worry, no doubt, no fear, and no was not an option, then what would you want?

Sadly, most people focus on and prepare for the worst thing that could happen to try to shield themselves from harm. People often use phrases like, "worst case scenario." If you even think about what the worst-case scenario would be, then what are you really doing? You are focused on the worst thing that could possibly happen. When that is your focus, that is what you will attract. Think about what you want instead and set the bar high. When you set the bar low then that is what you will attract.

Who would you like to become? What would you like to be doing, if you could do *anything*? How would you like to be seen by others? What would you like to do for your family? What would you like to do for your community? What would you like to do for yourself? Where would you like to live?

We are talking about you getting a very clear picture of who and where you want to be in life.

Do not focus on money. If you ask for money, you are asking for nothing. Money is a medium of exchange to get what you want. Focus on what you want. Money may very well be one of the ways that comes into your life to help you get what you want, but there are millions of ways that you can get what you want.

You hear some people go on about financial freedom. Maybe you're one of those people. If so, I have the quick three-step program to financial freedom that works every time:

> Quit your job;
> Move out of your house; and
> Live on the street.

What's that, you say—that isn't what you want? Well, it's certainly financially free living, isn't it? It is not enough to wish for freedom from financial difficulties. You must define what you are going to do, who you want to be when you are financially free. Focus on that picture.

This is a very practical exercise. Please write down the top five things that you would like to do, be, or have. List the big things, not the little things. There's no need to be shy. If there would were no limitations on what you could have in your life, what would those ten things be?

Write them here or on a sheet of paper:

1._____

2._____

3._____

4._____

5._____

Step #2

Are you with me still? If so, good job—now we get to the really fun part. The next step in this process is to ask yourself how you would feel if you achieved your goals. There is power in your feelings and in knowing those feelings. Focus on them.

Everything is energy: you, me, our feelings, that chair you're sitting on. Everything it means to be human is also energy. Our most powerful forms of energy are our thoughts and our feelings.

When you are thinking about your next vacations, what are the feelings associated with that?

When you are thinking about a new car that you plan to purchase, what are you feeling?

What moves you to take action and spend money (perhaps sometimes more than you want or should) is the direct descendant of your thoughts and feelings. Yes, you make financial decisions based on how you feel.

Think about how powerful that statement is.

I call these strong feelings your true heart's desire. Your true heart's desire is the thing you want most in life; it is the person you would like to become. When focusing on those feelings, you are focusing on the highest form of energy available to you, overriding all subconscious tendencies that you may have about not being worthy, about not being smart enough, about everybody else being brighter, faster, stronger, etc.

Concentrating on your true heart's desire is more powerful than all of the subconscious thoughts that hold you back combined.

It is important to note that your mind wants to keep you safe while your heart wants to move you forward.

Armed with your list of five things that you want to be, do, or accomplish, which ones of them really turn up the heat and get you excited?

For me, it is to play at Carnegie Hall. It has always been on my mind and in my heart. I intend to get there someday, even if I'm not the best musician in the world. Sure, some have said, "If you buy your way in, then it's cheating, and it doesn't really count." I say wait a second, who is making this rule? Is it someone who has actually played at Carnegie Hall or somebody who just wants to give his or her opinion? Honestly, if you have never been there, then should I be interested in your opinion on how to get there? What I care about is that I get there, no matter what it takes, no matter what method I use.

For you, the same thing applies. Focus on the destination. There are a number of different roads that will take you to your goal, and not everyone may agree on which is the best one, but the destination remains the same.

Just make sure that you pay close attention to your true inner feelings. Go through the list you prepared and really think about and feel each of your answers. Focus on your heart's energy during this process—that is the key to understanding what gets your blood moving. The more excited you feel about a particular answer, the better.

Step #3

It's time to measure the energy of your goals.

This step is works much like a Richter scale measures seismic energy. From 1 – 10, with 10 being the highest amount of energy possible and 1 being the lowest, how do you rank each of your goals? One thing to note about the Richter scale is that a 6 is ten times more powerful than a 5, and a 7 is ten times more powerful than a 6, and so on. When you get to 10 on the Richter scale, it is the be-all-end-all, so that is a huge amount of energy!

Rate your five items on the scale. Take some time, but really make sure to allow your heart to guide the level you rate each item. You may notice that a luxury car may only rate at 5 whereas, for instance, playing at Carnegie Hall rates a 10, or a good relationship rates a 10 and financial freedom only rates an 8. Get to know yourself through this process.

Many things that people wish for during times of lack spring forth as one gets closer to their heart's desires. For example, on my path to Carnegie Hall, if I get a luxury car, that's great, but I'm not focused on the luxury car. It's nice, but it's certainly not my ultimate goal. If it and other good things happen on the way there, I want to enjoy them, but they are not the big goals that register at a 10 on my Richter scale.

You should measure your feelings because, if you focus on what you want, then you will get what you want—but only when that feeling is strong enough to overcome your lacking beliefs.

It is important to remind you that 90 percent of our mind, which many people call the subconscious mind, is filled up with programming-based external forces from our environment such as parents, teachers, friends, colleagues, television, and media. All of it has programmed us.

If you objectively step back and look at this programming, you'll notice that it is primarily fear-based. Consider these statements:

> Save for a rainy day.
> Get a good education so you can get a good job.
> You need a steady job to pay the bills.
> You must work hard to get ahead.

As far as I can tell, the system of getting an education so you can get a job so you can stay employed for decades does not seem to be working anymore. It is extremely rare to find anyone who works for a company for 30-35 years, gets an amazing pension, and is happy as a lark until the day they die. These days, people are living longer, money is running out, companies fire people at retirement age, and governments are going deeper into debt. The old system—the old paradigm—no longer works.

By measuring your results, you measure your progress towards your goals, and you can tell immediately if you are moving closer to or further away from them. That is why you must measure your goals. It's all about keeping on track.

Rate each response from step #1 on a scale of 1 to 10 on the heart's desire intensity scale, where 10 represents 100 percent of your true heart's energy. (Number your desires along the bottom and rate them with a DOT on the graph.)

Remember anything less than a level 10 is less than good enough. No matter how long it takes, you must complete this exercise. You will find that, for the most part, you will only have 1 or 2 level 10 desires. If you rate all five things that you want at a level 10, then look at each desire specifically and really feel about each one. You will notice, more than likely, that one or two of them are stronger than the others. Remember, it is possible to get the things that are less than 10 as a natural result of going after the 10s.

Fig: 1 – The True Heart's Desire Intensity Scale

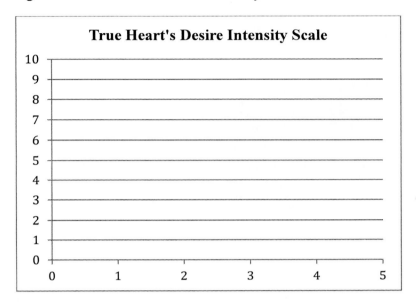

Knowing what you want to do, be, or have in your life is the first step to achieving it. If you don't know where you're going, you can't control where you end up. While you may have set goals before, there's nothing quite like knowing and connecting with your true heart's desire.

Throughout my life I have constantly created goals. Often, this was enough to get me close to realizing them and then... nothing. Success continued to elude me for many years. Goals are not enough. True heart's desires are.

To download a printable PDF worksheet of this exercise visit this url:

http://www.trainingbusinesspros.com/m/thdexercise

Chapter 7—Dubai

In the fall of 1994 I had the opportunity to go to Dubai, U.A.E., to perform with my jazz trio. Nancy was by now a full-time fixture in my life. The offer to perform at such an exotic location came through one of her work connections.

The original contract was for three weeks. We made such an impression that we were hired for an additional three months. This was of course a bit too long for Nancy and me to be apart, and so she quit her job and the two of us hopped on a plane to Dubai. This was our first opportunity to work with Hilton Hotels International and a tremendous shot in the arm for my career.

They say that everyone is famous somewhere, and I became a bit of a star in Dubai. From there we went on to play an additional six-month contract in Abu Dhabi, where we forged significant relationships not only with the Hilton hotel chain but with royalty, as well.

Nancy and I literally dined with royalty on several occasions. Looking back, I really didn't realize the connections that I had made and how much people loved the music that my band played. It was as though we were living like kings without actually having any money. Of course, the contract did pay very well, but certainly not the kind of money that the Emirates Royal families enjoyed.

The contract with the Hilton in Abu Dhabi was with a brand new private club called Hemingway's. This was the most popular club in the Emirates and was frequented by some of the most powerful people in the country. How I managed to forge these connections with these people and do nothing with them is beyond me. The fact of the matter is I knew nothing about business. Had I, I would've made something out of those connections. But, as I mentioned before, music was all that mattered to me—that, and we had tons of fun and lift a pretty upscale lifestyle. We were more than comfortable: The Hilton is a five-star hotel in Abu Dhabi in which we had our own suite, daily maid service, and all the five-star food we could eat.

Many great things came out of that trip. As an added bonus, performing almost every night of the week raised the level of my playing significantly. Everything felt magical, including my relationship with Nancy. She and I began to talk about marriage. However, she also in no uncertain terms made it clear that she was not going to marry anyone who did not know what they wanted to do. I always had dreams of being recognized as a significant musician in the jazz industry, and so I told her, "I want to be a successful jazz musician."

I am certain that, had I known then that the "true heart's desire intensity scale" exercise would be an integral part of knowing what I truly wanted to do, I would've been able to give a much more specific answer. However, I did not know of its existence yet, and consequently gave a pretty vague answer. How much more vague can you get than "successful jazz musician"?

I really didn't know of anything else I wanted to be. I loved jazz music. People loved it when I played, too. I visualized people wanting to come to my concerts just like they did Oscar Peterson's, Chick Corea's or Herbie Hancock's, my idols.

Of course, I was not nearly as good as them yet, but a guy can dream, right? Well, Nancy had faith in me. After returning to Canada after our contract in Abu Dhabi finished, we married the following summer. She became my full-time business manager and began the process of booking me concerts and festivals, and I started making albums.

I began the process of practicing very seriously and moved to Toronto where the prospect of becoming a recognized jazz musician was more likely than in Montréal. As soon as we arrived in Toronto, Nancy worked hard to make a name for herself as a jazz booker. She got a gig as the booker at a pretty serious jazz club known as Judy Jazz. Of course, it never hurts your chances of playing at a club if your fiancée is the booker. We also started to get some concert bookings. Nothing huge, but sometimes 500 or 600 people would come out for the festivities. Some of the more significant contracts included major jazz festivals in Toronto and Montréal where there were several thousand people in attendance. Let me be clear: We weren't getting rich by any stretch of the imagination, and fame as a jazz musician is always fleeting, but we were happy and floating along as best we could. We didn't have much, but what we did have was "good enough".

Until we got the itch for more, that is. It always comes—the want to try new things, to master new areas of life, to…well, make more money. Nancy and I decided to get into real estate and looked to purchase our first home. However, Toronto real estate is famous for being very expensive, and so we looked for quite a while to find the perfect opportunity. We purchased a small 1800 sq ft building. Okay, it wasn't really a house—more like a small office building. It didn't even have a kitchen or a shower. But with a little ingenuity, anything is possible.

I had always been good with my hands, and I bought some barn board off of my father, who had purchased it at an auction sale. I am proud to say that I built the kitchen from scratch. I'm not quite sure who would build a kitchen out of barn board, but I did. We really didn't have a choice. We certainly couldn't afford to buy proper cupboards.

We kept at the music business pretty seriously. I made album after album, pouring my soul into each one. Along with those albums came significant tours through Europe, Japan, and the

United States. I also played at several Canadian embassies throughout the world to showcase Canadian talent. The Department of Foreign Affairs and Canada Council for the Arts sponsored these tours. So, if I don't get the chance again, I would like to thank all those Canadians who pay their taxes.

Now, it may seem like things were okay, but the fact was that I was trading my time for money. If I didn't perform, I didn't get paid. This is the typical self-employed situation where many people find themselves in. If you are trading your time for money, then it's not a business; it's a job. Sure, go ahead and call it self-employment, but the reality is that you are working for yourself. You're not self- employed; you've just traded bosses.

It was a great time, but things were not as flowery as they first seemed. I was being paid great for the concert tours, but the reality was that I was barely breaking even once you took into account all the related expenses. We were actually falling behind! It seemed like this was a common thread in our money lives. Most of our friends had steady jobs, steady incomes, and could afford some of the finer things in life: nicer houses, nicer cars, and the odd getaway. On the other hand was me, with a beat-up car, an 1,800 sq ft office space to live in, and—besides the places where I got contracts to perform—there were no trips at all.

I was approaching 40 and, like many 40-year-old men, I was seriously entertaining thoughts of having a midlife crisis. But, of course, it's hard to have a midlife crisis when you have no money. How would you buy a car, take an extravagant trip, or do anything out of the ordinary without money? I certainly was no stranger to working hard. In fact, as you recall, that is the very message I had heard from a very young age: "Work hard and you'll get ahead." But the reality is that the harder I worked for financial freedom, the further behind financially I became.

Then, in the spring of 2001, everything came tumbling down... quite literally.

I will never forget the year 2001, because three things happened that changed my life forever.

During my seminars, people often ask, "What was the turning point for you?" My response to that question is a story that begins with 2001 and finishes with the statement, "I simply got tired of being broke and struggling."

The first significant event happened in the spring when I received official word that my new album, "Street Culture", has been nominated for a Juno award in the traditional jazz category.

On the outset, this seems like excellent news. I was excited, and everyone else seemed excited about it as well. This was the first recording that I had made as part of a record contract with Arkadia Records in New York, with whom I had signed the previous year. That record contract was for a total of eight albums—a pretty significant record contract, especially for a jazz musician.

Anyway, the Juno awards were to be held in St. John's, Newfoundland, that year. That meant that I had to get a plane ticket and airfare, which was next to impossible: It is expensive to fly to an island located in the middle of the Atlantic! So, being the enterprising person that I am, I applied for a Canada Council Grant to give a series of seminars across the country at University and College music programs. Of course, one of these universities would be Memorial University in St. John's. I would work it so that the seminar would happen at the same time as the Juno awards.

I got the grant, and I called the seminar, "I'm An Artist, That's My Choice." When I look back at it, I am floored by the self-serving title, and I wonder what the heck I was thinking.

Lesson—You-Focused Marketing vs. Me-Focused Marketing

Can you imagine naming something "I am an Artist, That's My Choice?" It smacked of hubris. Did anybody really care whether I was an artist or not? Would anybody really care about my choices? Not really.

As any good marketer will tell you, when you create a title or headline, you should always make it "you-focused, not "me-focused". Do you like having a conversation with someone who just talks about themself the whole time? Likewise, people don't like marketing that isn't geared towards them in particular.

Think of it this in this way: When you truly want to connect with other people, you want to make your marketing messages about them. That's what most people really care about, isn't it—themselves? For example, I would change the title of that seminar to something like; "Yes, You're An Artist: What Other Choices Do You Have?"

Getting into the habit of doing YOU-focused marketing instead of ME-focused marketing is your ticket to marketing success. It's always the What's In It For Me (WIIFM) question that you must answer. If you are only thinking about yourself, people will see right through you. That's why YOU-focused marketing appeals to audiences. You are looking for ways to help them, and that's what they want. This is a good lesson in Suggestology. Activating your reader's natural will to learn is more effective when you first strive to capture their attention. "You-focused" marketing certainly captures their attention far better than "me-focused" marketing.

Chapter 8—The Juno Awards

Picture a large hotel banquet hall filled with 1500 people sitting at roundtables and enjoying dinner. This was the setting for the 2001 Juno awards. My table was pretty much smack dab in the middle of the hall. At my table were the nominees in the three different jazz categories—that is, the ones who could afford to be there. Keep in mind that this portion of the Juno awards—the portion that deals with categories like Best Orchestral Music and Best Album Cover, etc.— is not televised. The televised awards showcases the most popular ten categories of the most popular music such as Best New Artist, Best Album, Best (-looking) Female Artist, and so on.

The announcer of the evening was Shamus O'Regan, the host of a popular morning show called Canada AM on CTV, Canada's biggest television network.

The entire night was abuzz with anticipation. Newfoundlanders are known Canada-wide for their partying ways, and so you can imagine how something as big as the Juno Awards coming to their biggest city brought that out of them. The place was hopping.

At some point in the evening came the announcement and the nominees for Best Traditional Jazz Album, my category. When they announced the winner, Mike Murley, a tenor saxophone player from Toronto, I was not in the least surprised. Mike had appeared on at least three of the nominated albums, including mine. In other words, he had a pretty good shot of coming out on top no matter what happened.

However, the thing that I remember the most was the reception of the audience during Mike's crowning moment. As he was called to the stage, they were underwhelmed, only a few dozen people giving the common courtesy to look up from their dinner to half-heartedly applaud. It certainly was nothing compared to the reception of some of the other categories. An entire audience of 1500 musicians and industry people couldn't care less about the jazz category.

It was at this moment that my life came together. It was as if a fog lifted. *What am I really doing here?* I began to ask myself some serious questions about my current status as a jazz musician and my future in the music industry.

I recognized that I shared three powerful personality traits with the other musicians sitting around my table.

a) We complained a lot. While this may seem like somewhat of a general statement and I'm sure there a few out there who suffer silently, most jazz musicians work very hard at their craft and recognize that most people do not understand what goes in to being a world-class jazz musician. Since all artists share a common desire to have their art seen and heard, it may come as no surprise that, when they are underappreciated, they complain. Also, they think they're smarter than most others. Granted, it does take a tremendous amount of skill and practice to perform jazz.

b) We all absolutely loved jazz. I have dedicated my life to the art of jazz and so had they. Even being recognized as a nominee in the traditional jazz category was an honour for me. However, when I realized that even a roomful of musicians couldn't care less about our life's work, I began to clue in to the fact that maybe I had chosen an art form that was not only dying but that may already be dead. How could I ever make a living with that form of music? That is, if musicians couldn't care less about it, how was the general public supposed to? I couldn't just selfishly pursue something that had no financial future—I had others in my life to provide for, Nancy and my young son Adrian, who I now had to consider in my decisions.

c) The last, yet most important, trait that we shared was; we were all broke. In fact, I looked around at the other musicians, most of whom were 10 – 15 years older than me, and I asked myself whether I wanted to be in that same financial position ten years down the line.

Needless to say, things were getting rocky for me.

Then, 9/11 happened. Besides the worldwide panic and horrible pain caused to thousands of New Yorkers, there was an aspect of the attack that hit close to home: Arcadia Records, the record company with which I had signed the eight-record contract, was within four blocks of the attack. They had to dissolve my contract, understandably: not only were many people afraid to come back to work in New York the months following 9/11, but people around the nation stopped buying anything, instead being glued to their televisions, frozen by fear. I'm sure the thought of stepping outside the safety of one's home or apartment to purchase a jazz album was likely the furthest thing from most people's minds.

So, as it would seem, this in conjunction with the events during the Juno awards spelled the near death of my career in music. Yes, perhaps hundreds of other jazz musicians were not nearly as affected as I was and continue to make their lives in music, but for me it was a devastating blow.

I can clearly remember the days, weeks, and months following 9/11, as Nancy and I started to have serious doubts about the music business and our future within it. In fact, we were immobilized with fear. Fear of the unknown. Fear of failure. Just a general fear of everything. Isn't it interesting that when you start focusing on what's not working that you start to attract more of the same? Not coincidentally, our financial situation was in dire straits and getting worse by the day.

Just as I was feeling down, questioning my ability to create worthwhile material that would sustain a family, something happened that threw my life into a whirlwind.

On January 6, 2002, at 5:30 am, my life changed forever. I got sick.

Two days prior to January 6, I attracted a particularly vicious head cold. The funny thing is that I rarely get sick. In fact, a major source of pride for me has always been my ability to ward off colds, flus, or any types of illness. Call it good genes, call it whatever you like— I just don't get sick.

However, I did get this cold. It stuffed up my nose. It made me cough. It had me against the ropes. On the second day, I also noticed that my ears were blocking up. It felt like descending in an airplane, when your ears feel like they need to pop. It felt funny and it felt different, but, to tell you the truth, I wasn't particularly concerned about it. I should have been.

In the early morning hours of January 6, I awakened with a loud, high-pitched whine in my head. It was almost as if I were sitting on the tarmac of Toronto International Airport and there were jets taking off all around me. The only other time I had perceived this loud ringing was after leaving a particularly noisy club, or maybe after performing jazz with a drummer's ride cymbal blasting away in my ears for three hours straight. But it was always temporary.

It was loud and seriously annoying. After about 15 minutes of lying in bed listening to it, I woke Nancy and told her I thought something was wrong.

" What is it?" She asked.

" I've got this loud ringing in my head and it won't stop."

" Well, don't worry about it. I'm sure it'll go away. Did you do anything to your ears, or hit your head? Or did it just come on all of a sudden?" She asked.

"I don't know," I replied. "I just woke up and there it was."

I really wasn't too alarmed at that time. I figured it must be just part of the head cold. But it didn't go away.

It got worse. Looking back on it now, I'm sure it wasn't getting louder but my perception of it as I focused on it created the thoughts of it continually rising in volume until I felt I couldn't stand it anymore. I lasted for two days until we made an appointment with the doctor.

After five minutes of examination, Dr. Koneiszna proclaimed that I had something known as tinnitus. In some cases it's temporary, but in many cases it is a permanent condition. *Permanent?* I was flabbergasted. What could be worse than a permanent obnoxious whine in your head?

"Please," I said to the doctor. "Isn't there anything you can do?"

"I can refer you to a specialist and then we'll see," she replied. The tone in her voice was not hopeful.

However, she gave me the name of a good ear nose and throat specialist, and I made an appointment that afternoon.

The next day, I went to see the ENT. The prognosis was exactly the same as the GP. It could be temporary or it could be permanent. But, in any case, there's nothing to do and nothing that could be done. The doctor advised me to go home and learn to live with it.

Learn to live with it?

This was devastating news. I began to panic. *How can they say that? Do they have any idea how invasive this is? Do they have any idea how I'm suffering?* "Learn to live with it"? Seriously, if you really want to knock the wind out of someone sails, then say something like that: "There's no hope, there is no cure, and you're pretty much on your own."

Well, the tinnitus didn't go away. And, as I suffered through the weeks and months, it only got worse. Much worse. I couldn't concentrate on anything: I couldn't practice the piano; I couldn't even carry on a conversation because there was this constant nagging high-pitched ringing that permeated every aspect of my life. The result? Depression.

Perhaps the pain of no recognition at the Juno awards was to blame. Perhaps losing my record contract contributed to the anxiety that I was feeling and as a result I brought tinnitus on myself. Perhaps tinnitus was payback for all the egotistical decisions I have made my entire life. Who knows? The only thing I knew was that the pain was real and the suffering was excruciating.

Over the next two years, I tried everything to reduce the ringing: prescription drugs, ear candling, acupuncture, homeopathic remedies, faith healers, dietary supplements, physiotherapy, massage therapy, shiatsu massage, and I even tried modifying my diet. Some of these brought temporary relief but nothing lasting and certainly no cure. As a last resort, I made an appointment with the Canadian Hearing Society, as I have heard that they were the countries leading experts in tinnitus.

They recommended something called "Tinnitus Retraining Therapy". The premise is fairly simple: you wear a hearing aid for two years which, in theory, produces white noise that can cancel out the noise of the tinnitus. Then, after time, you can slowly begin to reduce the volume of the hearing aid's white noise. After a long enough period, about two years, your brain gradually shifts to ignoring the tinnitus without the help of the white noise. Soon enough, you should be able to go without the hearing aid. At least in theory, that was how it was supposed to work.

The hearing aids put a significant financial burden on me. And they required constant attention. Things like fiddling with the volume constantly, putting them on, taking them off, cleaning them, storing them, changing the batteries, etc. Actually, the more I focused on using them, the more I attracted the need for them. My tinnitus volume never changed, and the entire exercise was not only regrettable but also completely ineffective.

Finally, after two years of struggling with tinnitus, I made an appointment with a doctor at the Musicians Clinics of Canada. This was a special clinic. It's designed to help musicians who suffer from repetitive strain injuries like tendinitis and/or hearing loss due to the constant exposure to loud music.

After only half an hour with the doctor, he proclaimed quite forcefully, "You, Mr. Tobey are clearly depressed. Do you have a drug plan?"

I thought this an odd question for a musician. Isn't it obvious that most musicians wouldn't have a drug plan? I mean, most self-employed people don't—so why would musicians? In any case I told him that I didn't.

"Because, I want to put you on antidepressants but they're expensive, can you wait here a minute?" He asked.

He walked over to a cupboard, kneeled down and proceeded to scan the many different drugs inside. He then grabbed a plastic bag and proceeded to put several dozen two-pill sample boxes into the plastic bag. He came back, handed me the bag, and told me to go home and take two a day for the next 30 days and then let him know how I felt.

I was actually quite pleased with this. I didn't really know that I was depressed and, truth be told, it was quite a revelation. I thought about this all the way home in the car. Could it be that maybe antidepressants could help me get back on track?

When I got home, I explained what had happened to Nancy and told her that these drugs were supposed to help me. And, I also quite happily gave her the prognosis and stated that anti-depressants were the cure.

And, at that point, I really could not have anticipated what happened next because I had never really been in that position with her. But she got very angry. In fact, I am quite certain that my attitude over the past years had not been exemplary and to her this was the last straw.

She screamed in a very loud and very serious voice, "if you take those, I'm leaving."

She went on. I remember it like it was happening right in front of me as I write this.

"If you take those pills, you will become dependent on them forever, and this is not the way to fix your tinnitus or your depression. You cannot fix something as serious as depression with drugs. And, if you insist on taking them, I'm out of here."

Wow. This, I had not anticipated. So, I got angry right back at her and gave her all the reasons why this was a good idea, but no matter how much I tried to explain it away, she either wasn't listening or refused to believe that pills were the answer.

I will never forget that moment, because it was when I broke. I got so angry that I flung my right arm towards the bottles of pills that were sitting on the table sending them flying all around the room. They landed everywhere. For weeks we were finding pills in the least likely of places. At that moment I broke down and cried. And cried. Then I cried some more. I had sunk to the lowest point in my entire life. My music career was dead, we had run out of money, I was seriously depressed and my tinnitus was never louder. Could things get any worse? Well, apparently they can. For, as I tried to come to terms with everything that happened and focused on what I didn't have, I kept sinking deeper into self-loathing, suffering, pain and depression.

Lesson—"Nothing great can come from no suffering." Eckhart Tolle

As you may surmise from my adventure with tinnitus, I am somewhat familiar with suffering. Now, as I look back to those dark days, I realize that anything that I have accomplished since then is a result of focusing my thoughts and feelings away from suffering

Because most people do not have specific destinations in mind, they lead their lives and make decisions by default. They are led around by situations and circumstances and, wherever they end up, they blame conditions beyond their control. Why? Because blame has a reward: It strips you of responsibility. Taking away responsibility for all the failures in your life? Now *that* is powerful motivation.

However, blame will never get you results. Neither will the justification that you are cursed or that you are unlucky, or that your bad situation is okay because others are in bad situations, too. The fact that other people have bad results may make you feel better, but it certainly won't change your situation.

And guess what? Complaining about your situation won't work, either. Of course, complaining is what most people do. Why? Because people feel bad for you when you complain; it feels nice to have people emote for you. It feels satisfying to have others feel sorry for you. However, just like blaming and justification, complaining about things won't change anything.

There were many circumstances where I could have chosen blame to make me feel better. I could blame society for not understanding jazz. I could blame myself for getting into an industry that I knew would result in little to no money. I could blame the terrorists of 9/11 for the disintegration of my record contract. I could blame the government for not supporting my career enough. And, most of all, I could even blame tinnitus for an affliction that caused immeasurable pain, anxiety, and disappointment.

However, that day when I batted those antidepressant pill bottles all over the room, I wasn't crying because I was sad. That was not the only reason. I was also crying because I realized that I alone was the cause of every negative thing that had happened to me my entire life.

I could justify my situation all day long by telling myself that maybe others were worse off and that there were likely thousands of musicians who were in the same boat. I could also complain about it to those who were close to me and even those that weren't. But, just like blaming, justification and complaining won't make anything better, period.

Perhaps you could think about it this way. Imagine for a moment you are an apple farmer. At the end of the growing season, you look at your apples, which represent your results, and you don't like what you see. Maybe they're too small, or worm-infested, or rotten. What would you do in this situation? Blame the weather? The worms? Would you blame the government, for not giving you enough farming subsidies? Maybe you could tack on some blame to the neighbouring farmer for not looking after their crops and allowing insects to infect your crops?

So, as you focus on your bad fruit and all the situations and circumstances which may have caused that fruit to become that way, you may or may not come to the realization that any blame that you could pass on to others will get you no closer to better fruit.

What could you do the next growing season to get better fruit? The first step is getting past the blame and asking this question. Think about that for a second.

Now, what is the one thing that you could do to strengthen the tree and get better fruit?

Focus on the roots instead of the fruits.

In other words, what you can't see is more important than what you can see. If you were to strengthen the roots of your apple trees, the likelihood of getting better fruit at the end of the next growing season would increase significantly. And, when you compare this to your life, if you focus on what's inside of you instead of the current results that you're getting, you can strengthen your inner roots.

What are your inner roots? They are what you think and feel. These are your spiritual beliefs. These are the things that neither you nor others can see, but they are real. Very real. In fact, in all cases, the things that you think and feel are responsible for the results that you've been getting.

Many people believe only in what they can see. They believe only in results that fit into their current model of reality. They are not content or happy with their reality or the results that they've accumulated in their lives. If you believe only in what you can see, then you will continue to create only what you can see.

I have learned that to create my life from the inside out is the only way to go. When I change the way I think and the way that I feel, I attract different results, better results. Sure, you can look at your reality and you can have complete proof of what you believe. If you believe that money is hard to come by, then you will find plenty of proof in your life to prove that you are right.

You will never have more money, but at least you are right. Right?

No doubt there are some doubting Thomases who would like to step in and say, "Hey, that's reality."

I say in response to that, "Reality is for people who lack imagination."

They don't say that the idea that money is hard to come by is reality because they understand how money works, but the opposite is true. If they understood money, then wouldn't it stand to reason that they would have come into some of it themselves? Create your own reality out of what you want to achieve, not what others think is impossible.

What are the things that you believe? What are the things that you feel? Do you constantly feel bad about the things that you do not have? Do you constantly feel the lack of money in your life? Do you blame others for your situation?

This is the basis of Suggestology: You must begin to ask yourself the *hard* questions. When you ask yourself these questions, only then can you activate your natural will to learn something. Then, once you have activated your will to learn, life will send you the opportunity to learn. But sadly most people will never do this. In fact, most people will spend their entire lives focused only on their results and what they can see. And they will not take any responsibility for the results that they have amassed. This may make life easier in some ways, not taking responsibility, but it will not make it better, nor will it change anything.

Perhaps it takes a tremendous amount of suffering before you begin to change. I have certainly suffered, and I'm sure you have, too. But was the suffering enough to make you change? How much more will you have to suffer before you decide that enough is enough?

Only until you acknowledge that you are not happy with your results, and only until you decide to change, will things begin to happen for you.

Suggestology is the art of asking questions. Ask yourself, "What would I be willing to do if I knew I couldn't fail?" That is a very important question. I have learned that no matter what I choose to do in life, the first step towards success in any realm is to take some type of action. Each time I try, I learn. Each time I learn, I add to my knowledge and experience. Eventually, as you amass knowledge and experience, you learn how to create something of extreme value. Nothing happens without action, and you can't modify your actions without actually having taken any action in the first place. You must step out of the comfort zone and take a risk. Remember the old adage, *the only risk in life is not taking one.*

What can you do now?

Stop the blame game. Stop the justification. And, most of all, stop the excuses and complaining. None of this will get you better results. There's nothing like your current results to tell you how far blame and denial have taken you.

Exercise—Stop the Complainathon

One of the most powerful actions that you can take in your life is to never complain to others about anything. Some people would explain this away by saying, "If I don't complain to others, then how am I going to get what I want?"

Yes, some people actually believe that complaining gets them what they want.

Sure, if you buy something and take it back and complain to the sales clerk, you will get your money back. That's not the type of complaining that I'm talking about. I'm talking about the complaining that you do day-in and day-out.

What you put out attracts like. When you complain, what do the people around you do? That's right: complain. Ultimately, it stops becoming a conversation and turns into one big complainathon.

What do you get from complaining? Ask yourself that. Think about it for a moment. Do you get others to feel sorry for you? If that is your payoff, then congratulations, others feel sorry for you. But, if you really think about it, how does that help you?

Are you complaining to others so that they can come up with solutions for you? That's not a good plan either. Why take advice from people who don't have what you want? Think about it. If you complain to others about money, and they are not wealthy, what kind of advice can you get?

I always tell people to never take advice about money from people in the same tax bracket as you. You might get different information than the information you already know, but it certainly won't change your financial situation for the better. All you will end up doing is moving sideways.

We all have well-meaning family and friends, but does that mean we should take their advice? Only if they can prove that they have experienced success in the area that you need help with. For example, if you are taking financial advice from somebody who earns less, the same, or even a little bit more than you, then you are taking advice from the wrong person. Taking financial advice from somebody who is broke is a really bad idea.

Your mission for the next 30 days is not to voice your complaints to others. Will this be difficult? Maybe, but I know you can do it. Be mindful. Monitor yourself. Pay attention to every thought that you have and when you are about to voice your thoughts to others in the form of a complaint, simply notice it, then stop yourself in your tracks. Noticing and acknowledging that you complain is the first step to change.

As soon as you voice your complaint, you have failed in the exercise. See how long you can go without complaining. Keep a record of your complaints in some other way. Carry around a notebook with you or keep notes in your smart phone. Write. Paint. Play music. However you do it, make sure that you do it without complaining to others. Go.

Chapter 9—The Pilgrimage

Have you ever heard of Oprah? If you live on planet Earth and own a television, odds are the answer to that question is "Yes". Oprah played a fairly major role in my transformational process. It's not that I watched her show or subscribed to her belief systems, because I didn't. But my wife Nancy did. Oprah had a guest author by the name of Gary Zukav. You may be familiar with Gary and his popular personal development books about the soul. Books like "Seat of the Soul" and "Soul Stories" were major sellers due in part to the fame garnered through his appearances on Oprah's hit show.

As Nancy was watching the show, some of the things that Gary said rang true for her, as did many of his ideas about how to attract a better life. That very day, she took off for the bookstore to purchase Gary's book, "Seat of the Soul".

Later that evening, she explained to me some of Gary's concepts and proudly presented me with his book as a gift, with the strong recommendation that I read it. It was obvious that her intentions were to fix me and she thought that this book could do it. I of course was not in the state of mind to read what I equated to as drivel. When you are in a state of denial, you do not read anything written by successful people. That would be an assault on your ego.

So, she read it herself. And she loved it. In fact, she learned many powerful concepts that still serve her on her journey. After she finished reading the book, she did some research on the internet and learned that there were soul groups throughout North America who get together and talk about Gary's work, its meaning, and how to apply it to their lives. Toronto did not have a soul group. She decided to start one.

She put out a notice through Gary's website that a new soul group was starting up in Toronto and, almost immediately, a lady responded to her post congratulating her and offering to help. Not only had this particular lady read all of Gary's books but she was also more than willing to offer up her own home as a meeting place for the soul group. Nancy was excited by this opportunity, and I was happy for her. What I didn't know was that she wanted me to go with her. I said there was no way

An hour of arguing later and we were on our way. With the directions and the address we ended up about three quarters of an hour later on the street in front of a very large house in a very exclusive part of town known as Bayview Village. This, I was not prepared for. Picture in your mind a row on both sides of the street consisting of luxury cars: Mercedes, BMW, Volvo. I was driving a beat-up 15-year-old Ford Taurus station wagon filled with rust spots. Talk about a fish out of water. Embarrassed, I parked as far down the street away from the house as I could. We got out of the car and walked towards this house, which was not really a house at all, but a mansion—certainly bigger than anything I had ever been in before.

We were greeted excitedly at the door by a 5' 2" Jewish woman in her early 40s named Laurie. She welcomed us with grace and warmth into her home. As we entered, my eyes drank everything in. Now this was living.

We then met her husband, Mark, who was a fair bit older than her, but just as polite and very friendly. The meeting consisted of about 20 people or so. The discussion surrounded personal development and Gary Zukav's books. The evening was certainly enlightening and, to be honest, I paid attention most of the time, but kept very quiet and back a bit from the group. Being outgoing is not something I knew how to do or had experience in. But these people were over-the-top excited and having fun.

After the meeting, Laurie came up to me and asked what my problem was. I thought that a very forward question and automatically became very uncomfortable, telling her that I didn't have a problem.

"Yes, you do," she said. "You seem depressed. You seem like you want someone to talk to."

Wow, did she have me pegged.

Laurie then led me by the hand into the library. I, of course, could never have imagined being in a house this size, let alone the wide, high-ceilinged room that made up her library. I mean, who has a library? She scanned the dozens of shelves while remaining quiet and, after a minute or so, walked to a shelf, pulled out a book, and put it in my hand.

"Here," she said. "Return it when you're done."

I had learned a little bit about Laurie throughout the course of the evening. People thought of her as intuitive; she was very spiritual. She seemed to be able to be whatever the situation called for—light-hearted and easy-going in a room with friends, calm but serious with someone who she is trying to help. I did not take her gift lightly—it was a tremendous gift and force for change in my life. In fact, I still recommend that book to almost everyone who crosses my path.

The book I'm speaking of is "The Alchemist" by Paulo Coelho.

It is a fairly simple story about a shepherd boy who goes out into the world in search of fame and fortune, but it blossoms into much more than that. It is a story of challenges and setbacks and how to overcome them, about recognizing and paying attention to intention. About staying committed to creating whatever you are in search of no matter the hurdles set ahead of you. It is the story of turning metal into gold.

For me, it was the first baby step on the road to transformation from a world of blame, justification, complaining, fear, and excuses to a world of limitless possibility.

For the next several months, I would go back to the Zukav soul group meetings with Nancy. Each week, I would return a book, discuss with Laurie what I had learned, and she would replace that book with a new one. I consumed books like they were candy. I realized my love of learning.

I was asking questions and diving into answers. I read many books on personal development from the likes of James Redfield, Deepak Chopra, Gary Zukav, Ekhart Tolle, Joe Vitale, Tony Robbins, Jerry and Esther Hicks, and many, many, more. This spiritual outlook was all new to me, but it was exciting. I began to feel much better about myself and about my ability to create change in the world around me. I didn't know what to call it then, but Suggestology was becoming a major force in my life.

Feeling positive attracts positive things and positive opportunity. Our financial situation was certainly not getting any better, but Nancy did get a job offer to be the director of the Park City Utah Jazz Festival. It wasn't a hard to decision. We packed quickly.

I won't go into all the details about Utah but I can tell you that you really shouldn't take the first opportunity that comes along. Why? Because, even though she did a great job and saved, in my opinion, that particular jazz festival from financial ruin, there were many things about Utah and the culture there that we did not understand or like. And six months later, we packed up our things and headed home. Because we had rented out our small office and loft in Toronto, we had nowhere to go. So, we found ourselves back in Brantford, Ontario.

The difference was, though, that we weren't broken—we were just broke. There's a difference between the two. In fact, regardless of our financial situation, I felt more positive than I had ever felt before. I was still feeding myself book after book. The diet kept me healthy.

After 20 years in the music business and financial failure, what was I to do next? What opportunities were to come, and what were the decisions I needed to make to move forward?

We placed our property in Toronto for sale and we did pretty well. We used the small profit that we got after paying off a significant amount of debt and invest it in a fair-sized Victorian duplex. It was in "the hood", but I didn't really care. The price was right.

However, "the hood" had a change coming. It's amazing what can happen when you bring a newfound energy to a street. Actually, people who were not even from Brantford purchased many of the houses on our street and they spent like we spent to fix these old places up and make them special. I've always been good with my hands and I worked with some local labour and trade people to get the old place into shape. We rented the upstairs to a young couple and their rent helped to subsidize the mortgage. It was a good move.

One of the books that I had read as a part of the long list of reading material given to me by Laurie, was another book by the same author who wrote "The Alchemist". It was called "The Pilgrimage". It was the author's own pilgrimage story that recounted how, in search of his sword as part of a spiritual ritual, he walked the "Camino de Santiago", or, in English, the "Road to Santiago". He talks about, in story format, how he met with several obstacles along the way and how he eventually completed his journey and found what he was looking for. It was an amazing read.

Personally, I thought it was all fiction. And, while it was a good read, it had been more than a year since I had read it, and I had filed it in the back of my mind under "interesting things I've read".

Was I ever surprised when early one morning during a visit to my father's hobby farm just outside of Brantford, in the small village of Burford, I saw the what the Burford Times was reporting. There, on the front page, was a story about a local citizen who had walked the "Camino de Santiago".

"It's real?" I said aloud.

After reading the article, which by the way was very detailed, I learned that the "Camino de Santiago" has been walked since the sixth century A.D. by thousands of people. In fact, thousands of people go there every year to walk the 850 km journey, starting in the Pyrenees Mountains and ending up in Santiago de Compostela where, as legend would have it, St. James (Santiago) is buried.

Somehow, I knew that I would take this journey.

What else was I going to do? After the death of my music career, I didn't know. What better way to figure it out then go on a walkabout? And what better place to do a walkabout than a journey walked by not only Paulo Coelho, but by hundreds of thousands of people over the past several centuries. In fact, many famous people have walked this road and went on to change the world in their own special ways: Dante, St. Francis of Assisi, Lorenzo de Medici, Anthony Quinn, Catholic Kings and Queens, the author and actor Shirley McClain (who also wrote a book about it), and many others.

I figured that if it's good enough for them, then it's good enough for me.

However, the flight, food, lodging and the right shoes were going to cost money that I simply didn't have. Still, I have learned that where there's a will, there's way. I remembered from my diet of spiritual books that, when you set an intention with deep commitment, then you will achieve that thing which you set out to do.

I applied for a grant from Canada Council for the Arts. It'd allow me to create music based on the inspiration of the walk, including the architecture, the people, and the history of the road. They turned it down. But, as I had done many times before when applying for grants, I simply changed the dates on the grant and submitted it again. This time, it was accepted.

The countdown was on. My plane was to leave April 30, 2004. Destination: Madrid, Spain.

Exercise—Walkabout

You must learn when you should push forward and when you should pull back and go on your own walkabout. It doesn't have to be across a foreign country. Just enough to take a load off. Most personal success trainers emphasize the fact that you need to fill your own well sometimes; otherwise, it'll run dry. Just like I had made the decision to walk across northern Spain, you, too, must make the decision to get away and recharge your batteries. There is nothing like a good walk in the country or in nature to recharge, revive, and replenish your energy.

Energy is everything. Walking surrounds you with natural energy and forces you to live in the "now". If you are overwhelmed, stressed, or anxious, then you are likely running out of the kind of energy that you need to accomplish your goals. If that is the case, then you need a good walk.

I still walk for at least an hour most mornings, on a trail near where I live. It allows me the opportunity to get out into nature and reflect on the blessings of living, focusing my intention, and the days to come. If there is no park near where you live, search out an inspiring destination of your own choosing.

Chapter 10—Last Test Before Spain

Spain would be the ultimate place to practice Suggestology. Everything would be new to me and therefore everything could be a learning experience. But even before setting one foot on that road, I was to face one last major challenge: an injury.

Two weeks prior to leaving, I went with some friends to Ellicottville in upstate New York for a two-day skiing weekend. And, while we had a great time, on the afternoon of the second day while navigating a particularly challenging diamond run, I felt my knee go out. My left knee has always been a source of trouble since a very early age when I was hit by a car while riding my bicycle. That particular day, it decided to give way. I cautiously negotiated my way to the bottom of the mountain and headed to the chalet, where I took my boots off and tried to get a sense of how badly I was hurt.

It wasn't that bad in the beginning. I could walk, albeit with pain, but it really didn't seem like it was going to cause any long-term problems. Even with my sights set on the Camino de Santiago in two weeks, I felt that I still had enough time to be in 100 percent top physical shape.

I was wrong.

The next day my knee swelled up like a balloon, and it got progressively worse over the next several days. I called my GP and made an appointment. His recommendation was to stay off it for at least a month and to then start physiotherapy. That was of course not acceptable, based on my commitment to walk the Camino. So, I asked him to refer me to a specialist, which he did. But, the specialist said the same thing.

I then called up a friend who is a holistic/ chiropractor/ homeopathic medicine man named Rolf. I figured if anybody could fix me, it would be Rolf. But I was again wrong. He worked on me right up until the day before leaving for Spain. His strongest advice was, of course, not to go to Spain but to stay home and let my knee heal. I explained to him that my ticket was non-refundable and, regardless of his or anyone's advice, I was going to go.

This was a real test of faith for me. I could barely walk and my knee was extremely painful. It was a struggle just to get from the car to the house, let alone walk 850 km across northern Spain. But the faith that I had built, the intention that I had created to do this journey, and the pull towards Santiago were incredibly strong. I had to go.

In the early morning hours of April 30, 2004 I hobbled to the airport.

Lesson—Deep Commitment

What's holding you back? Do you often make critical decisions based on the recommendations of others? And do the people who offer you advice and guidance actually have what you want?

If I think about the three doctors who gave me their recommendations not to go to Spain, the question I had to ask myself is simple: Have any of them walked the Camino de Santiago? In this case, the answer was no. No matter what their experience tells them, they had not experienced what I had wanted to experience.

Truthfully, most people would look at the source of the advice and think *Hey, these are doctors—you should take their advice.* Then again, you learn the most by trying something new.

Think about it. What is the worst thing that could happen? I wasn't being unsafe, really. I'm not much of a worst-case scenario kind of person, but let's say this: I get to Spain, realize that I can't walk half a kilometer let alone 850, and so I just take a bus. Or a train. Or, I might get right back on the plane and come home. Who knows? The point is, no matter what were to happen, it would be a good learning experience.

Everything in life that stands between you and what you want is called an *obstacle*. Do you let obstacles slow you down and even stop you? Do you let others dictate what you do? Can you not make your own decisions and take a risk once in a while?

I said earlier that the only risk in life is not taking one. To me, the only risk in getting on a plane and traveling to Spain was the fact that I might not be able to walk the road, but I might enjoy many other things such as the culture of Spain, the history, and even some of the locals. Maybe I could even pick up a little Spanish along the way.

It comes down to commitment. I was committed to going to Spain and, despite having no money and being told by several people who I respected not to go, I still made my way there, injury and all. What are you committed to?

Are you deeply committed to success? If not, any competing intentions will derail you. Perhaps you have been committed to losing weight in the past, but have also been committed to watching television every night while eating potato chips. Perhaps you have committed to earning more money, but are also committed to playing it safe by keeping a steady job that you hate.

There will always be competing intentions in your life. The question is; are deeply committed to the intentions that you've set for yourself? When you have competing intentions, only the one that you are deeply committed to will win out. My intention and deep commitment to get to Spain had been in the works for some time; I wasn't about to let a little competing intention like a sore knee stop me.

Brian Klemmer, a powerful personal development speaker, best-selling author and dear friend, said, "You can create anything you want in your life if you just follow this simple formula."

Intention + Mechanism = Results

Intention means making a promise to create something that you want to do, be, or have in your life that you do not have right now. But the only intention that matters is one that you are deeply committed to. As I've said already, only a tremendous amount of deep commitment will allow your intention to carry you through the obstacles that are set in your path.

Mechanism is a how-to. This is the strategy, the formula, or the tool that you use to carry out your intention.

These two things together will create results—any results—no matter how big your goals. However, any one part of this formula cannot work without the other. If all you have is intention and never take any risks or initiate any action, then you cannot expect results. On the other hand, if all you have are "how-to" strategies, then you are probably not deeply committed and have thus not created a strong enough intention to achieve your specific outcome. Brian Klemmer says, "If how-to's were enough, we'd all be skinny rich and happy."

If you look at your current results and you do not like what you see, then you must realize that you need a different formula. Perhaps this is the formula that you've been looking for. I for one know that it is! But, of course, how can you know it if you never try it?

The hardest part of this formula is deep commitment. If you do not have deep commitment to achieve something that you've never done before, then you likely will not achieve much. There will always be competing intentions.

How can you create deep commitment in your life?

Stop promising yourself that you will get there. You promised yourself before, and you've likely let yourself down. What are the consequences of letting yourself down? Nothing, really. There are no consequences except for the fact that you have not achieved what you wanted to achieve.

Instead of promising yourself, Brian Klemmer advises us to "promise someone who will be impacted by your failure." This could be a loved one, a business partner, or even a friend. Think about it like this: If you're not delivering, the people who count on you to deliver will be harmed in some way; yet, if you do not make a promise to them that you will deliver, then you don't realize the responsibility you have to finish what you're supposed to deliver. However, when others count on you, you promise that you'll deliver, and you do deliver, the universe will reward your selflessness and commitment to them.

If you truly want to create results in your life, then help someone else get what they want first, and you will have what they have in abundance. For example, if you want more love in your life, then help someone learn to love. If you want more money in your life, then help someone earn money. If you want better relationships in your life, then help others to understand what good relationships are. If you want peace in your life, then be a beacon for peace.

Exercise—Help Others, Help Yourself

Think about what you want in your life, and then think about someone else in your life who wants the same thing. Make a new connection with that person and help them get what they want.

This requires you to step outside your comfort zone and be a beacon for change in someone else's life.

On a piece of paper draw a line down the center of the page. On the left-hand side write the heading, "Things That I Want". On the right-hand side put the heading "People Who Want The Same Thing."

Even if you can't think of anyone who wants the same things as you, the intention you create by doing the exercise will bring those people into your life. Try it, and you'll see. That is the law of attraction at work.

I have noticed that my intention to create a training company and seminar business has attracted thousands of people who want the same things as me. Whatever the success that they're looking for, I can assure you that I want many of the same things as they do. And my intention to help them has created not only incredible results in my life but also in the lives of literally thousands of others who I've helped. There is no greater feeling than the knowledge that you have helped somebody along his or her journey! That is why I have written this book for you!

Chapter 11—Drew

I knew I wouldn't be alone on my journey across Spain. I knew I'd have some help along the way. And yes, while I could be metaphorically referencing the universe being aligned to support my intentions, I am speaking of something much more literal. I am speaking of Drew.

Drew came to me as a result of an ad. Once I received the grant from the Canada Council to write music inspired by Camino, I figured it would be a good idea to make a documentary about the whole thing. Nancy and I put out an ad for a director of photography to accompany me on my travels, and a man named Drew Dekker emailed me within minutes of my ad having been posted.

Drew was willing to pack up and go to Camino, and he knew Spanish. He had an impressive resume, including having worked for the Discovery channel. Actually, he had been working for the Discovery Channel filming ultra light aircraft in the mountains of Colombia, and a director of that film was an egomaniac. According to Drew, one day, while moving the crew from one film location to another, the director drove the chase vehicle several hundred metres into a live mine field. The whole crew were lucky to have survived and had to be airlifted out. That day, he walked away from the job. With no money and no way to get back to Canada, he ended up hitchhiking around South America for an entire year learning to adapt to the culture and learning Spanish. Perfect! Besides, anyone who can drive into a minefield and live to tell about it is my kind of guy. We hired him on the spot.

What I have been learning from books was starting to manifest itself in my life. I was attracting not only opportunities but also the right people for my dreams to become a reality. Many people talk about success as being in the right place at the right time. But as I was learning, it's about being the *right person* at the right place at the right time. The law of attraction was bringing to me opportunities to create. I realized that once you start looking for opportunities they would manifest themselves into your life—sometimes very quickly. I still had a lot to learn about success and was eager to learn, but it the power of what I had been learning and the strength of my focus to create reality were becoming more and more apparent.

Lesson—The Law of Attraction

The law of attraction states that what you focus on expands. Most of us have two areas of our brains that are constantly working: the conscious mind, which deals with the five senses and allows us to navigate through daily activities; and the subconscious mind.

The latter part of our mind makes up about 90 percent of our brain. This is the part of the brain that stores information and memory. All environmental factors affect this part of the brain. In other words, the way that you think and what you believe has been programmed into you by many external factors including family, friends, colleagues, teachers, media, and any other environmental influences that you have experienced.

The problem with the subconscious mind is that most of what you have been programmed to believe was inserted into your mind without much conscious thought from yourself during *the imprint period* (from newborn to seven years old). At this period of development, you did not have enough reasoning or cognitive ability to refute or dispute any false or potentially harmful beliefs. If your parents told you that money was hard to come by and you witnessed them struggling with money, then you likely believe that money is hard to come by and you are constantly struggling.

I have learned to believe that money is easier to come by than most people would lead you to believe. In fact, I have learned that it is possible to allow money to flow to me easily and effortlessly. However, because this is not most people's experience, many will try and convince you otherwise. However, look who is giving you the advice. You will find that most people around you constantly struggle. Perhaps you are struggling now? Think about what you've been told about money that might not necessarily be the truth, and consider who gave you your understanding of money.

At my seminars I am constantly asking my students what they've been told about money. Here are some examples:

Money doesn't grow on trees.

You have to work hard to get ahead

Get a good education and get a good job

Play it safe and don't rock the boat

Save for a rainy day

Most things are too expensive

Wait until things go on sale before buying

Are any of these sayings true? No. But that doesn't make them any less powerful. In fact, the law of attraction will prove to you that these things are true. But they are true because you believe only in what you can see. And so, if you see people struggle, and you are struggling, then you believe that you have to struggle and work hard to gain money.

What you may not know is that we are all masters of the law of attraction. This is both a frightening realism and a terrific opportunity. The law of attraction cannot distinguish between what is right and what is wrong; it only knows what you put your focus on. If you think you need to work hard to bring in the money, then—guess what?—you do.

Many people think all rich people are greedy. Expressions like these activate the law of attraction and keep you from being rich because subconsciously you do not want to associate yourself with being filthy.

How does Suggestology play a part in the law of attraction? If Suggestology is the art of activating your natural will to learn, how do you begin to learn and experience something like the law of attraction?

You need to change the way you look at things in order for the things that you look at to change. In order for you to activate suggestology within you, you have to begin to counteract your belief systems. For example, some people believe that rich people are all selfish—this is simply not true, and you must disabuse yourself of this limiting belief. The alternative is, of course, that you continue to hate rich people. But, you and I know that you cannot become something you hate.

Here is a radical yet enlightening thought. If you want to have more money in your life, stop saving money. I know—sounds weird, right? But the reality is that saving for a rainy day will bring a constant stream of rainy days. Why? Let me answer that with another question: When you save for rainy days, where are your intentions? Rainy days. You have focused on hoarding what little you have instead of earning. Your constant fear that money will run out keeps money from you.

No doubt this is a very difficult concept to grasp. I had a similarly hard time coming to terms with it when I was poor. But here's the truth: If you want more money in your life, you must allow money to flow *through* you, instead of stopping it when it gets to you.

Picture the flow of abundance as a river. Saving is like damming up that river. So, who downstream profits from the dammed river? The answer is no one. Why would you stop the flow of money when it gets to you? Saving it literally helps no one. Not you, not your family—nobody.

So why, then, are we bombarded with commercials and advertisements to save our money? Why are we constantly saving for retirement? Because we've been trained and programmed to believe that when you spend money it will run out. Get ready for a shocker: This is not true. However, because it is what most people believe, they will argue and present "evidence" to prove that they are right. You will always find physical evidence to prove your belief system. Which belief system would you rather be subscribed to? That's what I thought.

Exercise—How to Attract More Cash

In this exercise, we are going to counteract another one of your limiting beliefs. So, what can you do to practice the law of attraction to start attracting more money and success into your life? Once you have noticed your limiting beliefs and have started to counteract them with more empowering statements, then it is time to start taking physical action in the real world.

One of the actions that you can take, which will attract more money into your life, is to go to the bank and withdraw $1000 in cash. Put the money in your wallet or purse and carry it with you at all times. Ridiculous, you say? But how can you possibly be a millionaire if you can't keep $1000 in cash on you at all times?

When I first heard this from a famous real estate speaker named Dolf de Roos, I was more than skeptical. I was incredulous. However, he was rich, and I wanted to be where he was, so I took his advice. I withdrew $1000 and have kept it on me ever since. I spend it, but the first chance I get, I go back to the bank and replenish it. In fact, I did that just today. As I am writing this, a few hours ago I went back to the bank and added an extra $400 to my wallet, in cash.

Why would you do this? Because according to the law of attraction, you attract more of what you focus on. If you focus more on having cash, then you will have more cash? You will always find more at the bank in your account to withdraw. To most people, this would not make any logical sense, however, logic and reason have nothing to do with the law of attraction— at least with our current understanding of it. However, you use a light bulb without understanding the nuances of electricity, and still benefit from its resources. The subconscious mind is programmed like a magnet and attracts exactly what it focuses on based on what it believes.

Most people would say they would not keep $1000 cash on them because they don't want to lose it. What they're saying is *I don't trust myself. What if I spend it?*

If you want to live with money, you've got to learn to trust yourself in its presence.

Then, many people would worry about being mugged. What if it got stolen? What they're really saying is they don't trust others. Well, if you don't trust yourself and you don't trust others, who exactly is there left to trust? No one. And if you have no trust, you have no faith. And if you have no faith, you will always be broke.

And then there's a whole group of people who would say, "Hey! I have credit cards. What's wrong with credit cards?" What do credit cards attract? Debt. So if you want more debt, keep a lot of credit cards on you. The law of attraction is very specific. It will attract the very thing that you focus on regardless of whether it is good for you or not.

So, to re-cap: Your mission, should you choose to accept it, is to go to the bank first chance you get and withdraw at least $1000 in cash. Put it in your wallet or purse and keep it there for at least 30 days. If you spend it, which you should, go back and replenish it. At the very least, this will make you feel more successful, and when you feel more successful you supercharge the law of attraction. If you choose not to believe all this, then your belief system will prove to you that it doesn't work. However, try it at least for 30 days. What have you got to lose?

Even if you did lose it or had it stolen, will $1000 ruin your life? Not likely. And what are the odds of losing it and having it stolen? About the same odds as getting struck by lightning. Of course, don't be stupid and spend it frivolously or wave it around in public. Keep quiet about it, and just feel the law of attraction bringing more cash to you. This may be a difficult step for you to take, and it may require a lot of faith in yourself and this project you've undergone with me. But I've guided many people to their own paths of abundance; I am a weathered Sherpa, and I will guide you to your goals. However, while it is *simple* to become millionaire-minded, it may not be *easy*. You have to question your belief systems, change them to align with your intentions, and take chances. Now, off to the bank with you.

Chapter 12—A Journey Of A Million Steps Starts With Step One

In the late evening of April 30, 2004, Drew Dekker and I, after a long flight to Madrid, a train to Pamplona and a bus into the mountains, stepped out into a small village called Roncesvalles, located high up in the Pyrenees. I'm not exactly sure what we were expecting in terms of the weather, but it was cold, damp, and there was snow on the ground. We were most certainly underdressed in t-shirts and shorts. I'm sure we had visions of Spain at the end of April as being a warm summer-like vacation destination. Oh well. We quickly searched our backpacks for our jackets.

The bus left us standing there and drove off. There were three or four ancient stone-structured buildings in this very small village and no signs of life. We agreed to split up and look around. I went to one of the buildings to the south of the road while Drew headed off in the other direction. A few minutes later I heard loud whistling coming from Drew's direction. I turned to find him about 100 yards away, standing in front of a large barn-like stone structure with smoke billowing from the chimney.

I limped slowly towards him, as my knee was really killing me after being cramped from the lengthy bus trip. Slowly I caught up with him, and the two of us cautiously entered the building.

Have you ever walked into a place where everyone stopped what they were doing to stare at you?

We entered the doorway and about 30 or 40 people turned towards us. It was then that we realized that there was something different about our new friends. We were dressed in summer clothes while everyone else was decked out in the most modern, tough-looking hiking gear imaginable. There were backpacks, hiking boots, and other gear strewn all over the place. These people looked serious. They were also German and at first glance nobody seemed to speak English. Someone pointed to a couple of bunk beds in a corner, and Drew and I took our gear over to the corner and placed it on the bunks.

This was our first encounter with other pilgrims. Needless to say, it was a pretty humiliating experience. I'm sure they all must have seen us as true novices who didn't really know what we were doing. Which of course, was true.

That night we slept soundly as a result of a very long day in planes, trains, and automobiles. I was nervous about the walk ahead and fell asleep thinking about my knee. Was it going to support me, or was it going to make me look like a fool for trying? It could go either way. But, after all of my readings, and all the personal development ideas and exercises that I had already implemented and saw take fruit, rather than think the worst, I imagined the best.

Lesson – Worst-Case Scenario

People often think and prepare for worst-case scenarios. In other words, they set the bar low by imagining what the worst-case scenario might be and then take action based on that being their destination. Most people set the bar low because they do not want to be disappointed. It's a way of anticipating failure and avoiding disappointment, because how can one be disappointed with something they've expected all along?

Of course, setting the bar low may shield you from disappointment, but you will never get what you want. Why? The law of attraction will give you what you focus on. If you focus on what the worst-case scenario might be, then you will attract just that, worse, or (if you're lucky) a little bit better—but you will never attract a big win. Do you think a hurdle-jumper even wins a race by focusing on the obstacles in front of them?

The only way to win or achieve anything big is to set the bar high! Nothing big ever got created with small ideas. When you set the bar high your focus and attention is put on something that you truly desire. And, what I've realized is, more often than not you will come very close or even exceed your expectations.

Even worse than setting the bar low is subscribing to what is known as "Murphy's Law." This law states that what can go wrong will go wrong. I'm sure that Murphy believed wholeheartedly in this law, but I don't. Of course you will find plenty of proof that this law is real if that is where you put your focus and that is where you set the bar. Your expectation is that things will go wrong and therefore you will attract the very thing that you set your expectations on.

Your mission in life should be to set lofty goals and go about the process of achieving them. Do you think for one second that Thomas Edison set out to make a light bulb that would last only 10 seconds? No, of course not. He set out to create a system of perpetual light that would shine for generations, and he succeeded. If he had set the bar low or given up after creating a light bulb that lasted for 10 seconds, you and I may have never known electric light. And Thomas Edison was not a God. He was a person, with flaws and doubts like you or me. But he didn't give up on himself, he didn't express doubt through actions, and he constantly innovated his approach to reflect the best-case scenario for his experiments.

Winners always set the bar high and then learn what they can along the path to their destination. It's not always a perfectly straight line to their destination, and so they adapt to each and every obstacle. Remember, it's only a mistake if you make it twice. So, from now on, challenge yourself by setting the bar high and adapting to the obstacles in your path. You cannot learn anything by setting the bar low and shielding yourself from disappointment. If you continue to persist in lowering your expectations you may of course never be disappointed in the short-term, but you will never get what you truly want, and that is true disappointment.

When my eyes finally opened after a deep uninterrupted sleep, I found Drew standing on the ground beside me with his head right next to mine. I was on the top bunk, and his eyes were at the same level as mine. He told me he thought it was time to go.

"Why do you say that?" I asked.

"Because everyone's already gone."

I sat up in bed and looked around the fairly dark room and noticed that, out of the several dozen people, only a couple were still there, and even they were packing the last of their sleeping bags and clothes into their backpacks and heading out the door.

I knew before I went to sleep that we had a deadline of 8:30 am to vacate this particular Refugio, and so I asked Drew what time it was.

"It's 7:15 am," he responded.

"Where did everybody go?" I asked with a confused look on my face.

"I guess they've already hit the road. I think they want to get to the next Refugio before all the beds are taken." Drew explained.

"Hmmm, so we should hit the road too?"

"Uh, ya. Let's go."

My mind was immediately drawn to my knee. I cautiously made my way off the top bunk and put my leg gingerly on the floor... It held. It was sore, no change from the previous evening, but at least I could stand on it. We got dressed, brushed our teeth and headed out the door. After a moment, we were back inside, fishing the raingear from our backpacks.

Cold. Damp, too. Drew decided to walk 100 yards or so ahead and set up his camera to get the first walking shots of my journey across Spain. I remember very clearly those first steps. I had a walking stick to support my left knee and I very cautiously headed down the path. Most of the trail was your typical goat path, plenty of trees with pine needles and leaves spread out across it, making it spongy beneath the feet. There were certainly areas that were rocky, craggy, and steep. I took my time that first day. Most of the other pilgrims had reached their first destination Refugio within about seven hours. The first leg of my journey was closer to 17 hours. We were so late in arriving that, sure enough, we could not find a place in the Refugio to sleep. Now I know why everyone gets up so early and rushes to get out on the trail. It's a race to see who gets the next beds first.

Anyway, I had heard that about a kilometer down the trail was another, less-busy Hostel, and so we headed there.

After finding a set of bunk beds and taking off my backpack and hiking gear, I sat down at a table and ate some food that I had picked up at a small grocery store along the way. After an hour of sitting, I tried to stand up.

I was clearly in pain. My knee had swelled significantly during the day, and there was no ice to be found.

I was talking about this with Drew when a lady there noticed our conversation and said, "I think I can help you with that."

She said she was a performer of Reiki healing. I didn't know why a complete stranger would help—or try to help, at least—me with my knee troubles, but I figured it couldn't do any harm.

She had me lay on a table and for the next half-hour focused her healing powers not only on my knee but on other areas of my body as well. I know many people who practice Reiki and swear by it. For certain the mind is a powerful thing, and I do truly believe that, when focused in the right direction, it can speed healing and even cure.

"Thank you," I said to the woman after our Reiki session. "If there's anything I can do for you, please let me know."

"You're welcome."

I never saw her again. She disappeared on the road just like the vast majority of other pilgrims whom I met at one time or another.

Now, I'm not completely sure how much her healing had helped, whether it was the energy of the Camino itself, or whether my focus and attention was completely directed on reaching my destination, but here's what I can tell you: Four short days later, my knee was at full efficiency. No pain, no swelling. It was completely mobile.

Four days, that's it. Do you remember the three doctors who had told me not to the chance of going to Spain?

I couldn't believe it. If this was the power of the Camino, then what else was I going to learn from this journey? If I could heal a very significant and painful knee injury in just four days while walking close to 100 km, what laid in store for me ahead?

Exercise—Meditation

There is no such thing as stressing the following point too much: When you focus on what you want, you will attract the very thing that you put your focus on. One of the more powerful ways that I have learned to focus and attract is through meditation.

Yes, I completely understand that many people believe that sitting peacefully in one place, calming the mind and renewing your energy, is a waste of time. In their minds, I'm sure they believe they are right. However, I prefer results instead of being right. And meditation has always helped me focus and stay grounded.

Did you know that scientific studies have now confirmed that meditation is beneficial for the human body? This age-old practice is no longer something for sceptics to pooh-pooh; the fact is that business owners and billionaires who know what's good for them meditate every day.

If you are not familiar with how to meditate allow me briefly to explain how it works.

Basically, all you do is find a quiet place where you can be alone. Sit comfortably in an upright position and loosen any clothes that feel tight. Place your feet squarely on the floor, close your eyes, take deep breaths, and focus on your breathing. Relax every area of your body. I like to do it in order: I start from the tip of my head and slowly relax everything until it reaches my toes. This includes my eyes, ears, chin, cheeks, neck, shoulders, chest, stomach, hips, thighs, knees, shins, ankles, toes, and everything in between. To focus on each one of these pieces of your body is to relax them one-by-one and to completely filter out the influences and stress that life places on you.

I highly encourage you to download one of my personally directed meditations by navigating to web page I'm about to give you. This is a great way to learn how to meditate and to be directed into a peaceful and calm state. Meditation is proven to relieve stress and anxiety, and it can help to ground and center you, preparing you for the opportunities that will come your way.

Meditation will also attract opportunity by allowing you to clearly focus on the outcome instead of what you don't want. Here is the URL to download our meditation. Please copy it into your web browser exactly as is:

http://www.trainingbusinesspros.com/m/meditation

Chapter 13—Slow Down, Pilgrim, Slow Down

With my leg healed, I was ready to take on the world. My excitement took the better of me, and, foolishly, I decided to join the race for the next bed. I had learned that not getting to the next Refugio before some of the other people usually meant travelling longer in search of other places to sleep. In some cases that meant walking to the next town miles away. And, after an entire day walking, an extra five km walk is the last thing you want to embark on.

Being part of the race to the next Refugio meant, of course, walking faster. One particular leg of the journey was fairly long and there were no resting spots between the starting and ending point. Word had reached us that the destination Refugio was not that big—certainly unable to take in more than 40 people. Judging by the number of people who were at the starting Refugio, there were at least 50 on the move with us. Drew and I decided to wake up early to get an early lead on the travelers, around 6 am, and get started. By that time, most of them had already left. We decided there was no time for breaks.

The destination was the city of Burgos. We started from a bed bug infested Refugio, formerly a monastery in a town called San Juan de Ortega. That day's walk was to be 27 km but the last few kilometers were quite steep downhill. We were feeling pretty good and confident that we could get there on time. We were walking fast, catching up, when, all of a sudden, in my right heel I felt a snap.

Immediately, a sharp pain shot through my right heel. I tried to walk, but every step was excruciating. I yelled for Drew to stop.

Even though I thought it might have been worse, I told him it was a sprain, and that he would have to help me walk.

So, I put quite a bit of my weight on Drew's shoulders and we hobbled the rest of the way into town. We did get to the Refugio on time and found a couple of bunk beds that were free. Half an hour later the entire place was full. I rested that evening by reading a book and went to sleep early. The next morning I tried to stand, but couldn't.

The rules of the Camino are that you cannot stay more than one night in a designated Refugio. Therefore, Drew and I had to find a hotel. We stayed in that hotel for a couple of nights until I felt strong enough to put weight on my ankle and continue the journey.

Those three days that I spent in Burgos were some of the most productive, creative moments that I spent on the entire journey. I ended up composing three entire pieces and starting a fourth. One of those pieces is called "Burgos Bossa Nova". It's one of my most favourite pieces of music. It was completely inspired by the music of Burgos. There was a street festival going on at the time and plenty of live outdoor folk music. The folk music of this area of Spain is a mix of traditional Spanish, Latin, and modern dance music. It was very inspiring. I would go on to arrange that piece of music for entire orchestras.

What I learned is this: When you look for evidence faster than the universe is willing to give it to you, strategic obstacles in your path will slow you down. I've learned that often the quickest way to your destination is to just slow down. I could have been sad that I had to stay at Burgos. Instead, I took it as a sign and sowed the seeds of creation. The universe wanted me at this time to compose music. Burgos was the perfect place to stop and become inspired. The universe knew that before I did and my ankle injury was not only a message but also a gift.

Lesson—Seeds of Creation

I'm sure you have enough common sense to know that when you plant a seed in your backyard you don't run out the next day, dig up the seed, and demand to see immediate results. No, you let nature take its course. You plant the seed, water it whenever possible and eventually it turns into the very thing that you want to create: a flower, a plant or even a tree. That is all I mean—that, just as you let nature take its course, sometimes you must allow universe to take its course, too.

People tell me all the time, "Paul, I'm busy and I'm overwhelmed."

"Doing what?" I reply. Are you always busy? What is it that you really have to do? Why are you in such a hurry to get things done? And what are all the things that you have to get done?

Stop trying to figure out exactly how you will get to a certain destination. Set an intention—plant a seed. Then, whatever the universe decides to throw at you as obstacles, stay calm. Those obstacles are meant to either slow you down or divert you in a more appropriate direction.

Because we want to have complete control over everything, we see obstacles as problems to solve. But this is not always the case. You cannot solve a problem with the same mind that created it. If the mind that created the problem was in a hurry, you cannot solve that problem by using a mind that is in a hurry. Therefore, sometimes problems exist in order to guide our minds to a new place. Slow down, take a deep breath, and notice what the universe is trying to tell you.

Most people believe that the only way to reach their destination is to work hard. There are literally millions of ways to reach any destination that you choose, so how could you think there is only one? That is simply not true.

Only when you detach from the specific outcome that you had intended will you get to where you want to get more efficiently than before. Is there a law that governs this particular aspect of your personal development? Yes. It is called, aptly, "the Law of Detachment."

The law of detachment goes something like this: Focus on what you intend to create and you will attract opportunity, however, you must completely detach from the outcome. In other words, knowing that there are many paths to your destination, try not to focus on only *one way* to your destination; allow the universe to deliver you the opportunity that it sees fit.

This is where most people would say, "Hey, this is my life we're talking about here. I wanted that business deal. I wanted things to turn out this specific way. I wanted to earn that contract and that amount of money. I had my mind set on getting that job." I completely understand that this goes against the programming that you have been given, but that does not make the law of detachment any less effective. The law of detachment is as real as logic and reason. However, logic and reason have nothing to do with the law of detachment. Only when you learn to let go and let things happen will you feel more calm and relaxed than ever before. Then, when you are happy and feeling peaceful, you will attract more opportunity and more success.

Many people ask, "What is the quickest way to get from where I am to where I want to be?" Funny enough, the answer is to stop trying to figure out how you will get there.

This is likely the hardest lesson that you will ever have to learn in life.

When something happens that you did not intend to happen, you must learn to accept it. Acceptance does not mean putting up with the things that you do not want in your life—doing that is a form of resistance.

What does acceptance mean? It means having a quiet inner knowing that your intentions are being carried out to the eventual fruitfulness of your intended results. You not expect that results will come exactly as you plan. When you detach from the idea that results come exactly in the way that you plan, only then will you get results faster.

You can see now that, for many people, this does not make sense. It does not comply with their belief system. In fact, most people do not believe that you should "let go" and let things happen. They misunderstand what it is to detach: Of course you must take action, but you must also completely be okay with whatever result you get. Only then will you begin to supercharge the law of attraction and bring results to you at light speed.

The problem for most people is that when they set their sights on a specific outcome, their focus is usually only on the one way they can perceive to get it.

For example, let's say you want to take a vacation. The way most people would go about that is to pick a time that they are off work and then save up the money to go on the vacation. And while that seems like a logical strategy, there are a million other ways that your vacation could come to you.

If we focus on a specific path, strategy, or plan to bring something about, when it doesn't happen exactly as planned we become upset, agitated, worried, and fearful. We let it trip us up. It seems natural to do that. That's the way we've learned. We were taught that if we work hard, then we would get ahead.

That's the only way, right? My question to you is," How is that working for you?"

If you are going to really understand the law detachment, then you're going to have to go much deeper than just thought. Most humans would think their way to a result when in actual fact they should be *feeling* their way there. Every human possesses a massive amount of creative magnetic energy; humans are ultimately creative, every one of us. And we're also magnetic: We draw situations, circumstances and people to us based on how we feel.

The law of attraction and the law detachment are intertwined. When you detach from any specific outcome, you feel better, and you know that life is supposed to be effortless. And so when there is effortlessness about life and you are feeling good, that activates the law of attraction, which then brings things to you quicker than if you were to try and force them.

The law of detachment is uncommon in today's world. Most people have either not heard of it or have heard of it and dismissed it because it's not part of their belief system. I once had a gentleman send me an e-mail after a seminar saying that he did not believe it was a good idea to make money while you sleep. He said he was from the old country where they work hard for their money. The question I asked him is, if he had been working hard his whole life and still had not got felt like he had reached many of his goals, then isn't it time for a different plan—a better strategy?

My belief system says the law detachment is the quickest way to get from where you are now to where you want to get. By all means! Pick a specific destination or a specific goal. However, when you take action, and you must absolutely take action, don't be surprised if the very path that you wanted to take has several roadblocks in the way. And rather than force yourself through them, the law of detachment is very clear on what you should do: Stop, reassess, reinitiate, and take the opportunity that seems like the easiest route.

This is not the normal way to behave. But there is nothing normal about extraordinary success. If you want extraordinary success, you will eventually have to understand, practice, and utilize the law of detachment in your life.

To be sure, the law of detachment is not putting up with the things in your life that you do not want; the law of detachment is initiating and taking action towards a big goal, but then detaching from whatever path and opportunity that is sent to you to achieve that goal.

You literally have to revamp your entire belief system. It is difficult. I suggest that you either pick up a book and read more about it, and there are several out there, or take a training seminar with somebody who understands this law and can give you specific exercises on how to make it come about.

A perfect example of the law of detachment is this very article. Every morning I set out on my walk with my digital recorder, not knowing exactly what I want to write. I just know that I will write something. It doesn't have to be perfect and I don't have to strategize for six months on an article. I do not have to force the contents to come, but I simply allow the meditative act of walking to bring into my mind something that feels good and to dictate that into the recorder.

I have written hundreds of articles, but I'm sure that those articles would have never been written if my mind got in the way. Knowing exactly what you're going to write is the biggest detriment to getting anything done. And usually when someone tries to write exactly what is planned, they generally never get started or never finish, because it always has to be perfect.

The hardest thing that I've had to do in my life is to understand the law detachment because I am inherently a perfectionist. However, I can tell you that when I let go of the need to be perfect, which is an ego-driven concept, things flowed easier into my life, and for this I am grateful. My greatest wish for you is that you understand the law of detachment, and at least initiate some steps to bring it into practice in your life.

Exercise—Practicing the Law of Detachment

Many people think that detachment means putting up with the things in your life that you do not want because that's just the way life is. That is not detachment, but resistance. Try to think of it like this: if you are unhappy with your current financial situation, but at the same time say to yourself, "Things could be worse" or "Everybody has financial problems", then you are in resistance. Putting up with something that you do not like is resistance.

The law of detachment is wanting something without needing it.

Here is a quick little exercise that you can do right now to test how much *allowing* you are capable of and how much you are *detached* from the outcome.

Think of something in your life that you are unhappy with. This could be a relationship, a financial situation, a problem at work or even something that needs fixing or replacement. Picture the situation clearly in your mind. Play it as a movie in your head. Visualize in as much detail as possible exactly what you are unhappy with. Can you see it clearly?

Take a deep breath. Now imagine it turning out exactly the way you want it to turn out. Whatever the problem was is now fixed.

The problem has disappeared entirely. Try to envision the situation, with you in it, and it has now been completely corrected. Visualize the situation as clearly as you can the way you would like it to be. Take another deep breath and allow the situation to right itself.

Your ability to visualize the intended outcome without actually stressing about it or worrying about it is detachment. Imagine that you do not have to do anything that you do not want to do for the situation to correct itself. If you can do that, then you are allowing the situation to be corrected by itself. The opportunity to create the perfect situation cannot come to you unless you can visualize it and detach from the outcome. You must let go of your attachment to the outcome before you can see the outcome.

Success can only come to you if you do not need it.

While you are envisioning the perfect outcome, you are in a meditative state. When you are focused and in a meditative state you will begin to attract whatever it is you desire. The reason why a meditative state works better than just thinking about it is because a meditative state signifies to the subconscious that you are calm and detached. When you are detached you will attract.

Chapter 14 - Santo Domingo de Silos

A few dozen kilometers past Burgos began the vast flat expanse of the Meseta Plains. Whoever said, "the rain in Spain stays mainly in the plain," has obviously never been to Spain. It was hot and sunny every single day.

The several hundred kilometers that it took to cross the Meseta made Drew and I lean, tanned walking machines. It was an opportunity for me to put my hiking boots in my backpack and wear sandals with smart wool socks. Am I ever grateful I took those sandals: While everyone else's feet were hot and sweaty and blistered, mine felt perfect.

Some of the highlights of this three-week journey included the monastery ruins at Castrojeriz, the medieval Festival at Hospital de Orbigo, and performing for a music school in the fairly big city of Leon. Drew and I were enjoying the journey. We did get lost a few times, but eventually got back on track and before we knew it were climbing up the Galician Hills to Cebreiro.

One of the things I remember most about Galicia is the strong, sweet smell of the eucalyptus trees. As you get closer to the West Coast and the Atlantic Ocean, the trees become more abundant and strong-smelling. About 150 km between Cebreiro and Santiago de Compostela, it is only about eight legs of the journey and eight days from the official and of the Camino de Santiago. I knew that we were going to walk another 90 km past Santiago to the coast, but still, I could feel the end drawing near.

We had originally scheduled more time for this journey than was actually needed, because I didn't know how my knee was going to react and how much time it would take to film footage for the documentary, but in the end we found ourselves with extra time. Heeding the lessons from Burgos, we decided to slow down.

I stayed three days in Sarria, two days in Portomarin, and an extra day in Gozo between Arzua and Santiago de Compostela. Sometimes the universe can slow you down on purpose and sometimes you can make the decision to slow down and enjoy the journey yourself. That last week or so before Santiago was really enjoyable. I managed to write quite a bit of music and even score an entire orchestral piece based on the piece of music I had written early in the journey called Caminar—Spanish for "walking".

Before we knew it, we were taking those last steps down the mountain into Santiago de Compostela. And, as we approached the official end of the journey known as Santiago's Cathedral Square, we were overtaken with emotion and the history and power of the towering ancient structures.

The cathedral itself is without a doubt one of the most beautiful structures I have ever seen. It is a fantastic Romanesque exterior and a Baroque architectural masterpiece. It is highly ornate inside and adorned with thousands of religious icons, art, and sculptures.

It is tradition on the day of arrival by pilgrims to receive your *Compostela*, the certificate of completion, as a symbol of a complete pilgrimage. There is an official office where you receive your written and signed Compostela, and there is also a pilgrims ceremony and ritual in the great cathedral.

It was a particularly busy tourist day in Santiago. The weather was bright and beautiful and there were thousands of people milling about. Drew and I decided to get to the cathedral early so that he could set up the camera and film the ceremony. He scoped out a particularly advantageous spot and we captured some extremely brilliant footage. The ceremony itself featured a hymn and symbolic words, and prayers by Catholic priests. The highlight was the giant swinging incense burner known as a *botafumeiro*. It is a long rope that hangs from the high dome and half a dozen men cling to the road and swing it high to the eaves. It is quite a sight and tremendously moving.

After the ceremony we exited into the cathedral square, which has a large fountain and is made completely of golden granite. I stood atop the tall steps of the cathedral looking over the square when I noticed a familiar face. It took me a few seconds to clue in, but standing 50 metres from me was Nancy.

I turned to Drew and he just shrugged his shoulders. He obviously knew that she was coming and didn't tell me. It had been just over a month and a half since I had left Canada and, even though I had spoken to her several times on the phone and had communicated by e-mail, it was obvious that she missed me enough to travel all the way there by herself.

We hugged and kissed in the square for several minutes. It was quite an emotional moment, but eventually I started asking a few questions like, "How did you get here?" And, "Drew, how long have you known that she was coming?"

It turns out that Nancy had flown into Bilbao and rented a car.

The next morning we packed up the tiny car she had rented and headed directly east on the exact same road that we had walked in on. What had taken us 6 1/2 weeks to walk took only one day to drive. We even stopped at several small towns along the way to share with Nancy some of our experiences and some of the history of the road.

One of the things that Drew and I didn't get to do, because it was several kilometers south of the actual Camino route, was visit the famous Benedictine Monks of Silos. So we decided to visit and, after arriving in Burgos, we headed south to the Abbey of Santo Domingo de Silos.

The monastery of Santo Domingo de Silos is extremely famous for its very old and very beautiful Romanesque cloister and, of course, for the Gregorian chanting of its monks. The monks have made several recordings of their music and at one point became very popular when, back in the 1980s, they released an album of their chanting with a rock music rhythm section.

The highlight of this visit was being allowed to film an interview with Padre Ramon, one of the more senior monks at Santo Domingo de Silos, while walking in the famed cloister adorned with Romanesque and Baroque architecture. We were told at the time that this was the first and only video interview within these famous walls. The reason we believe we were granted the interview was because of our special status as people who had received their Compostela.

The interview with Padre Ramon was tremendously eye opening. Not only did I learn a lot about a monk's everyday life but also their philosophy, history, and spirituality. We chatted about their lifestyle and the future of modern-day monks.

To watch this special interview, follow this web link.

http://www.trainingbusinesspros.com/m/the-brotherhood

Lesson—Peace

What is it that we can learn from Padre Ramon's message? How can we filter the message for use in our everyday life? Personally, I think the message is about peace. How can we work together to create a world in which there are no more conflicts and no more wars? Padre Ramon speaks very clearly about this in our interview.

Perhaps the message for the purpose of our goals is to use Suggestology as a means of communication. Rather than trying to be right, should we focus on asking the right questions of each other? If it is truly possible to live a peaceful life, then you must be constantly questioning those who know how to live and promote peace. Perhaps your message to the world should be one of peace.

One day, after several weeks of hard work, a farmer decides that, because it is such a beautiful day, he will hitch up the horses to the wagon and head into town for some supplies and human contact. The trip into town would take about three hours and so the farmer spent a bit of time preparing provisions and getting everything ready. Soon, he was heading down the long laneway and out to the main road, which lead to the nearest town.

His faithful dog quickly took up stride beside the wagon, excited to explore new territory. The dog darted from side to side across the road, diving into bushes, disappearing into the forest, jumping into the streams, and basically tearing all over the place. As the farmer witnessed this he wondered what had gotten into the dog, but figured it was simply excited and curious.

Not too much later the dog completely disappeared. The farmer didn't worry about it, though, as the dog was known to disappear, sometimes for hours on end. Soon enough, the farmer reached the town, tied up the horses, and went up the steps and through the front door of the local Mercantile. He's greeted by the shop keeper with a great grin.

"What can I get for you today?" asked the shopkeeper.

The farmer pulled out a list and, one by one, the shopkeeper started putting the supplies together and tallying up the totals. They were just about to finish up when the dog struggled in through the front door. The dog was completely winded and thirsty, as evidenced by his heavy panting. His hair was all matted and muddy, he was bleeding from one leg, and if truth were told he seemed to be on death's doorstep. The shopkeeper looked at the dog and said to the farmer, "My, that must've been some journey!"

To which the farmer replies, "it wasn't the journey that got him, it was all the rabbits he was chasing."

Ask yourself what the rabbits are in your life that you are chasing.

Most people have entire communities of rabbits in their lives. The rabbits are metaphors for distractions. Everything that you have to do, all the places you have to go, and all the duties and responsibilities that you take on represent your daily activities and distractions.

Please take notice of the triangle below. Figure 1. The vast majority of people represent the largest portion at the bottom of the triangle. These are people who have a constant stream of activities and distractions in their lives. The question is, does this bring you success? In most cases the answer is no. In fact, the more distraction that you have in your life, the less likely you are to pick a new destination.

Then, every once in a while you may meet up with somebody who inspires you to create some goals. This represents the next level and smaller group in the triangle. Many people at some point in their life create goals. The challenge with this system is that goals create a whole different set of activities and distractions. In fact, the bigger the goal that you create, the more activities and distractions will accompany it.

Then there are a small number of people who live at the top of the triangle. This represents people who have purpose and a message. Very few people reach this point in their lives, where many of the things that they do is for the benefit of others. Have you stopped to examine why it is that you may not feel like you are living a fulfilled life?

Fig 1.

The answer may be, and likely is, that you do not have a big enough purpose. In fact, if you did have a message for the world, what would it be? Then, it is not enough just to think about it— you actually have to take action. What would be the action that you could take?

Maybe you could start coaching others and giving information and advice based on your experiences.

Maybe you could join a charity or group of people who through their collective decisions and actions benefit others.

Perhaps you could write a book.

One of the things that I found to be the most beneficial in my life was to step outside my comfort zone and make it not only a point to help others but also my solemn duty and responsibility. That is the goal of this book—to help you get something new in your life that you do not currently have.

Whatever you decide to do, I can guarantee that when you make a portion of your life about other people, you cannot fail. The universe will always reward your action and any action that you take towards the benefit of others. The funny part is that others do not need to be affected for it to work. All it takes is the intent to help and some type of action. Many people have tried to help others in the past and have failed. Yet, those people still feel the pull of purpose in their lives and are benefited by simply creating an intention and following through.

Exercise—Following Through and Becoming a Magnet for Opportunity

Whatever you want in life, take the opportunity to help create it in the lives of others.

Write down on a piece of paper three things that you could do in the next 90 days that could benefit either an individual or a group of people.

Then, beside those things, create a list of actions that you could take that would solidify the intention.

Then, follow through with at least one of them.

One of the biggest challenges that almost everyone faces is following through. This does not require a huge action on your part, but it does require you to do *something*. As long as you take some type of action, there will be a reward for you in the form of opportunity. Do not look to the people who you give to for a direct reward from them. You will be rewarded, but not necessarily from them.

Whatever your purpose and your message for the world, take the opportunity in this lifetime to create it. However daunting this task may seem to you, your life will be completely fulfilled if you do. All you have to do in the next 90 days is to take one single action that benefits others. You'll be glad you did because you will feel great. And when you feel great you will be a magnet for opportunity.

Chapter 15—The End of the Earth

The next day we packed up the car and left Santo Domingo de Silos for the airport in Bilbao. The trip took us only a couple of hours. The three of us talked about the things that we had learned not only from Padre Ramon and the entire monastery experience but also the Camino itself and our journey together.

The next thing I knew I was saying goodbye to Nancy at the airport. It was a whirlwind three days and I'm sure that she regretted having to leave, but we had a five-year-old at home and other obligations. It was an emotional parting, but I assured her that a few weeks later I would be home. After that Drew and I dropped off the car at the rental agency and walked to the train station, bought some tickets and headed back to Santiago de Compostela. The journey seemed to go much quicker than the car ride, and before you knew it we were carting our backpacks up the stairs at the main pilgrim's Refugio.

The following morning Drew and I were back on the Camino heading towards the ocean. The lush green foliage of summer was in full bloom and the smell of eucalyptus trees wafted through the humid air. There were far fewer pilgrims for this part of the journey as Santiago de Compostela is the official end of the pilgrimage. There were only about 10 pilgrims at the first refugio. Everybody spoke of their journey on the Camino and their reasons for continuing on to the coast. The young people in charge of this particular refugio offered a very special *paella* meal for only five euros. If you are not familiar with paella, it is a mix of shrimp and vegetables over rice. They baked it in the traditional way—in a giant skillet over an open fire. This is one of the few meals that I actually remember from the two-month journey, and it was delicious.

Four days later, as we emerged from the mountainous areas of Galicia, we could finally see the ocean. It took a few hours from the time we could see the ocean to where we could actually smell it. Most of the journey had been hot and dry, but this particular day it was overcast and windy. Pretty soon we were walking along a beach towards the small town of Finisterre. The name of the town, directly translated to English, means "End of the Earth". Before the New World was discovered, Finisterre is geographically the furthest point West in Europe, which explains the quirky name.

Finisterre is a small fishing village on a rock peninsula that juts into the ocean. There is only one official refugio there, but it is reserved only for pilgrims who walk the Camino, like we had. We checked in during the late afternoon and had a quick nap and then, at dusk, all the pilgrims who had arrived that day made the two km journey from the town to the lighthouse on the coast, which represented the very last stop of the Camino.

There are three things that pilgrims are supposed to do when you get to Finisterre: Take a bath in the sea, burn something at the lighthouse, and watch the sunset from the lighthouse.

It was a bit cold that evening, so I reserved bath time for the following day when the sun came out. It was much warmer then. However, that evening was a very sentimental time: a time for reflection, a time for stories, and a time to think about going home.

One of the pilgrims lit a fire and several others took off their socks and burned them in the fire. Drew took his socks off and threw them in the fire, as well.

"Thank God," I said. If you had to smell those socks every night for the past 60 days you would want to burn them as well!

To see my final thoughts on video, filmed that very evening in Finisterre, please visit to the following URL.

http://www.trainingbusinesspros.com/m/finisterre

Exercise—Little Rituals and Celebrating Your Successes

What happens when you reach your intended destination or you achieve a goal? Do you celebrate your success? One of the things that I learned from the rituals of Finisterre is to *always celebrate your successes*. No matter how big or how small they seem to you, take the time to enjoy and celebrate. This will raise your level of energy and prepare you to receive further reward. I realize that for many people it sounds silly to celebrate every little thing that happens, but you must. This will make you a much happier person and will allow your energy to flow quickly towards many other good things in life.

Some of the things that I have learned to do, which are small rituals, are giving and receiving high-fives, hugs, lunch or dinner on the town, a day off, golf, vacations, buying a book, going skiing, out for coffee, or even on a long walk. No matter what your little rituals might be, you must do them. If you don't have any little rituals, create some. The more you celebrate the more you will attract greater success. Do not discount your success and shrug it off. Be present, participate wholly, and celebrate wholeheartedly in your successes.

Chapter 16—A New Canadian is Born

When I had arrived back in Canada after being away for two months, it was the middle of summer. The first thing that everyone noticed about me in Brantford was that I had lost literally about 30 pounds. At 6'2" I was a virtual beanpole. I can tell you that it's almost impossible not to lose weight on a journey like that one. I had lugged a 50-pound backpack 850 km across Spain. I was deeply tanned and felt very strong, but that didn't stop people from telling me that I looked too thin.

I had been thinking about my future during those last few weeks in Spain. I still didn't have a clear picture nor did I have any real goals in mind, but I can tell you that I felt great—better than I had felt in a long time. My tinnitus had calmed considerably and, while it was still ever-present, it didn't bother me nearly as much as it had in the past. Financially, Nancy and I were not doing well at all. Even with the grant money taken into consideration, I had spent far more on the journey than I had intended. And, after being away for two months, it took me a little while to get back into the swing of things and find ways of making money.

As a dedicated and committed person to the music business, I had learned many skills out of necessity, which everybody knows is the mother of invention. For example, I had learned to build my own websites, record and edit my own music, film and edit video, score music, and I was pretty good with computers. As a result of this, from time to time I would help other artists and even small business people build websites and do their computer work.

I had always been pretty handy with computers since University, where I minored in computer science. This was actually an accident; I had originally signed up for political science, but after one extremely boring political science lecture, I found myself in the registrar's office cancelling that course and picking the only available one—computer science. Even though the computer languages that I was learning, like COBOL and FORTRAN, would eventually become nearly extinct, I still learned a lot about how and why to use computers. They didn't scare me. I used them always to my advantage. My personal belief system is that computers make things easier and do tasks that would be literally impossible to complete without them.

A few weeks following my return from Spain, I received an e-mail out of the blue from my dear friend Laurie. You remember Laurie, the Jewish lady who had started and sponsored the Gary Zukav soul group meetings? Well, through her connections, she had learned of an interesting video project started by a husband and wife out of England. In essence, the project was a DVD-of-the-month club for people who were looking for more positive messages in their lives. It was a spiritual project of sorts, and it was meant to inspire and motivate people.

The founder of the project called "Closer to the Dream" was a man by the name of Terry Malloy. Terry was passionate about this project and had quit his managerial position at the bank and leveraged his house to start it. He was looking for someone who could do many of the things that I could do: someone to edit video, compose original music for each segment, build a website, handle e-commerce. Terry even offered to pay me to include segments of my own, such as my documentary from the Camino de Santiago. It seemed like the perfect project and paid better than I had imagined.

When you put yourself out there, opportunity appears. I was excited about the project and about the prospect of creating original material and music and utilizing my web design skills. It was a bit of a long-distance relationship with the company as they were in England, but the communication process through mediums such as Skype kept things moving forward. There were other people involved in the project, such as a film director in California and a few other talented people, but I had a major role. I worked very hard to make sure that the first DVD and the website were of high quality. I spent quite a bit of time writing music and editing my documentary over the next few months. And, because this website was bigger and more important than any project that I had done before, I spent long hours and worked late many nights to make sure that everything was as good as it could be. I am a bit of a perfectionist, and I wanted to make sure that I held up my end of the deal.

One thing that bothered me about this project, however, was the fact that, while I know a lot about production and could certainly create a product of high quality, I didn't know if it would sell. I mean, think about it—a DVD-of-the-month club with each and every DVD being original high-quality content. That takes a lot of money and a lot of time. I wasn't sure whether the project was sustainable without a lot of money coming in. So, even in the early stages of production I would ask Terry, "how are you marketing this?" I am certainly not a marketer, and I told him so. I was concerned. But Terry, being the very highly spiritual person that he claimed to be, would say things like, "Don't worry about that. It's going to be a fabulous product and everyone will want it."

It didn't take a genius to realize that unless we sold a lot of these things, Terry was going to run out of money pretty quickly. But he just kept saying that a lot of people would be interested and, while we might not sell that many in the beginning, it would be sustainable and would grow over time. I'm not sure I believed him, but I was getting paid to do a job, and so I did my job. In hindsight, I probably should've questioned the system a little bit more as I really felt inspired by the project and wanted it to continue for as long as possible. It was a fantastic outlet for my creativity and I was really enjoying myself.

Next thing I knew, the entire first DVD was created, printed, and I was sent 10 or 15 copies by mail. They were beautiful. The packaging was exquisite and I quickly opened one and popped it into my computer and played it. It wasn't perfect. There were certainly many things that I would change the second time around, but I really felt that it was good enough for a first time offer.

We had decided on a launch date sometime in the fall of 2004. I can't remember exactly when that was but everyone was looking forward to getting down to it and getting some sales. I had tested my website over and over again. I had made sure that the site was secure and that the ordering system functioned properly. Again, I'm not really a marketer and didn't know anything at that time about how to convince someone to sign up for a monthly DVD, but I did my best and took a lot of guidance from Terry about how to construct the website and what it needed to support the project and make sales.

When the launch date came, I replaced the "under construction" homepage image to the entire website and just like that, we went live. I'm not sure what I was expecting. I didn't really know anything about Internet marketing. I had never even heard the term before this project! So, I didn't have ways of monitoring traffic, and even if I did I wouldn't know what to look for. But what I did notice is that after 24 hours of being online, no one signed up. Not one person.

I had a phone conversation with Terry the next day. He wasn't nearly as confident as he had been in the past but who assured me that this was the early stage and not to worry. He claimed that it takes a few days for people to talk and the sales would start to come. But they didn't. In fact, two weeks later the only two sales that were made were test sales by Terry himself.

I know that it took a lot of capital to get that project to the point where it was. I wasn't too sure of Terry's financial situation, but it didn't take a genius to realize that a lot of money had been spent and no money was coming in. I had put hundreds of hours into this project and was still owed several thousand dollars for my work. At this point, based on the sales numbers being zero, I started to get really concerned about getting paid. In hindsight, this should not have been my concern as for me it was only my time that I had on the line. Terry had hundreds of thousands of dollars on the line. So when I inquired about his financial situation and when I would get paid, my questions were met with swift condemnation.

Perhaps I was to blame for not building a website that was very market-friendly. Perhaps I was even to blame for making an inferior product. But, from my perspective, I was not hired to market the product, I was hired to build a website and make a project. I was not a salesperson and never purported to be a marketer. That's why I asked Terry several times what his marketing plan was. In any case, I received a multi-page letter soon thereafter.

The formal letter from Terry detailed the reasons why I wasn't going to get paid, and it shifted a lot of the blame, most of it in fact, to me for the project failing. I was devastated. Every spiritual bone in my body started to ache. I thought that I was in attraction mode. I thought that I was starting to get very familiar with how to attract opportunity and realize success. I had read that success is not about being in the right place at the right time, it's about being the right person, in the right place at the right time. I was obviously not that person yet.

I took the failure of this company very personally. In fact, for several months I went in to saviour mode and tried to rescue the project, the company, and Terry. I didn't really do it because I felt I was to blame; I did it because in my family you help. You work hard and you get things done. Regardless of everything that had happened, I was going to learn what was missing and try to fix it.

I had faced this same situation many times in my music career. Every album that I had ever made was done with the same amount of care that I put into this project. But, just like this project, many of my albums didn't sell, either. Sure, jazz music represents a very small percentage of overall record sales, but that doesn't make it any less discouraging when you have a basement full of unsold albums. In this case I'm sure that Terry had an entire house full of unsold DVDs. I felt like I had a duty and responsibility to step outside my comfort zone and learn how to sell them. I had no idea how to do this, but I knew that I had to learn if I was ever going to make any money in this world. Marketing for an artist is a very difficult thing. I had always felt like it was somebody else's responsibility. Not this time.

And, just like every other opportunity that I had attracted in my life by focusing on what I wanted, I got down to the business of focusing on marketing. This drive led me to a competitors website, the Spiritual Cinema Circle. Essentially, it was the same type of company as Closer To the Dream. Started several years earlier by a famous film director named Stephen Simon, they had a proven system and a viable company. If you don't know Stephen Simon, he directed several famous films—most notably a film with Robin Williams called "What Dreams May Come."

Stephen had an epiphany one year when his wife went in for routine surgery and ended up in extended psychiatric care. He had built a wonderful company and I can even remember going to a seminar of his in Toronto one time. A brilliant man, a wonderful director, and a great businessman.

While scanning his website one day, I noticed a link in the bottom right-hand corner, it was a link to something called an "affiliate program." When I first saw that I didn't really know what it meant so I clicked the link. The webpage that I landed on talked about how you could join their affiliate program and get paid to send traffic to their website. You wouldn't get paid for the amount of people that visited the site but you would get paid a commission if anyone sent by you bought the product. This was an interesting concept. What if I could get the same affiliates as they had to send traffic to the Closer To The Dream website?

On that webpage it listed a few of the top affiliates. One of them was a gentleman named Tony Indomenico, who lived in Australia. I thought about it. *How does somebody living in Australia become an affiliate for a company in California?* So, I picked up the phone one night and called him.

Tony was a real gentleman. He explained to me the ins and outs of an affiliate program and how it works. He also told me that he made a significant amount of money from the spiritual Cinema Circle program as well as other products and services that he was an affiliate for. This was intriguing to me, because it seemed like he was earning a lot of money just for sending traffic. I asked him, "Do you think you could send some traffic to our product?"

"Of course. I'd be happy to." He replied.

That response made me very enthusiastic. I began to think of ways to entice other affiliate marketers to this project and maybe even save Terry's house. Who knows, it was worth a shot. Tony and I agreed to meet via Skype each night for the next several nights. In essence, he had agreed to mentor me in the ways of the Internet, something for which I had very little experience but was willing to learn. The reason he did this was because he was building some projects of his own and he needed some video, music and website design. It seemed at the time that was another fortuitous opportunity that I had attracted.

And so, over the next several weeks I not only learned a lot about affiliate marketing but it set me on a new path to discover things like search engine optimization, copywriting strategies, joint venture partnerships, auto responders, and many other internet marketing concepts. Our discussions also led me to other sources of information. I began to get really excited because I finally was learning a system that could be used to market and sell not only Terry's product but my products, as well. Maybe I could figure out a way to even sell the CDs in my basement!

I came across another source of marketing information called Nitro marketing. It was started by a couple of young men in their early 20s named Kevin and Matt out of Austin, Texas. After reading through their website and the many learning products that they had to offer, I picked up the phone and called Kevin.

This was a very interesting discussion. I inquired not only about their marketing systems but also if there was money to be made as a marketer. His response? "Millions."

I was not quite prepared to hear that. It didn't make much sense to me, how all that money could come just from streamlining information and acting as a middleman who attracts business to customers, but it did make logical sense. I knew I would do okay at it if I were able to make money selling something—anything—with new system I had studied.

Lesson—"An Investment in Yourself Is the Best Investment You Can Make." -Benjamin Franklin

The best thing you can do is invest in yourself, but more than half of Americans never do. Did you know that 51 percent of North Americans have never read a nonfiction book past high school?

Think about that for a second. 51 percent of us feel that we got all the learning we needed to get in high school. That means we relied entirely on high school teachers to give us the balance of our knowledge. I'm not saying that high school teachers are not smart, but they certainly don't know everything. Like many of us, they, too, are just a couple paychecks away from ramen soup and homelessness. The fact is that if you want any success in your life at all, you will likely have to invest in information.

Obviously, the best type of information to invest in is by someone who not only has a great system but who also has a proven track record of implementing that system. There's nothing like learning from someone who has experienced what you would like to achieve. Many of my online learning systems not only talk about the things that you will need to learn to achieve success but many of the things that I've learned that do not work.

Don't think that just because you have a good idea that all it takes is a little trial and error to come out on top. That's what Terry thought, and things weren't looking good for him. The biggest problem with trial and error, aside from the error, is that it takes a really long time. The quickest way to your destination is to find somebody who's already there or past where you're headed, and then learn from them.

Exercise—Make the Investment

Your mission for the next 90 days is to find an online learning system or seminar that you can invest in and learn what you need to learn to get to your next destination. One system that I highly recommend to start making money selling anything you want online is my own system, entitled, "12 Essential Lessons on Internet Marketing". I have taken the best pieces of advice from the many professionals I have spoken to and combined it with the knowledge which my experience has afforded me to craft this lesson plan for you. You can find it at the following address:

http://www.trainingbusinesspros.com/m/12-lessons

Activate Suggestology in your life, accentuate your natural learning ability and become a learn-it-all.

Chapter 17 - Bad news is good news…?

Unfortunately, during the same time as I was learning internet marketing, I was not getting paid and not working on anything else in particular. As a result, our money and credit literally ran out, and the bank came calling. We had to put our house on the market. I had spent quite a bit of money and a lot of time over the previous two years renovating this property into a viable duplex, but this neighbourhood was not known for its high listings. We put a lot of sweat, tears, and money into renovating the whole place—leveling out the floors, replacing walls, everything. The place sparkled when we finally put it up for sale, hoping it would help us start the long trek to getting back on our feet.

It sold on the first day that it was listed. For the highest amount that any house had ever sold for in that neighbourhood! We had purchased it for $138,000 and sold it for $230,000 in just two years.

After settling our consumer debts, we could barely afford another fixer upper in the same neighbourhood. It was just a few blocks away, and it needed a lot of work. However, by now we were experienced with working on houses! I had learned quite a bit about construction by renovating the last two, and I figured we could do it again. We took the leap and bought it.

After only three weeks of owning the place, we started smelling something awful from the basement. We went downstairs. There, hidden behind a stack of musty boxes, was a doorway.

The doorway led to a space that opened up the front one third of the house. This room was floor to ceiling with dirt. We found out that the front part of the house was built on a small two-foot foundation and on top of dirt. Lye had been tossed on top of the dirt to keep the mould (and who knows what else) under control.

It smelled really bad. We immediately called in an expert to assess what we were up against, while kicking ourselves for not having sprung for a building inspector.

Turns out, the front part of our house wasn't just stinking, but sinking. Everything was a little off-balance. After the inspection, the engineer quoted us $65,000 to fix the problem. More than half what we paid for the house. And the kicker was there was no saying no—the engineer said the house would have to be condemned if we didn't go forward with the construction.

There was no question about one thing: We certainly couldn't afford the $65,000. A few sleepless nights ensued.

Finally, we decided to do it ourselves, and to hire some local help to assist us in rebuilding the foundation. We scooped up a couple strapping young lads from the local orphanage. We also had another renovator helping out, a guy who had helped out on our last property. It was hard work, and the hours were long.

In the end, the total cost of the project including labour was $6,000. Where there's a will, there's a way.

While all this was going on, I continued to work late into the evening and sometimes into the early morning hours. I was learning how I could possibly make money online not only to save the Closer to the Dream project but also to make money selling anything online. My work area consisted of a makeshift table up against a plaster and lath wall which was literally cracked and crumbling. The carpet was filthy and looked like it hadn't been changed in over 30 years. In fact, when we eventually lifted the carpet, it took us two weeks to scrape the rubber from the back of the carpet, which had moulded itself permanently to the floor. Only heat guns and scrapers were able to remove the carpet.

Fall was coming. We had to get the main floors of this house renovated so that we could finally get our bedrooms straightened around to the point where we could live comfortably. Pretty soon it was Thanksgiving and we were invited to my parents for dinner.

Because of the state of our house, we decided to stay overnight before driving back the next morning. When we arrived back at our house the first thing we noticed was that the front door was partially open. Oh no.

I quickly parked and ran in the house thinking the worst. I scanned the main floor where I had spent countless hours on my computer only to find the entire computer system gone. Not only that, pretty much everything was gone, including TVs, tools, electronics, some furniture, and much more.

Still, the only thing that I could think about was my computers and backup hard drives. Gone. My entire life's work—gone.

Everything I had ever created had been transferred to digital format and was on my two main computers and backup drives. I thought that I would be the last person someone would steal from, being close to destitute myself. I was wrong.

It took over an hour for the police to come and after a brief discussion the officer gave me an incident number and told me to call my insurance company. Basically, robbery is low on the priority list with the police department, and he essentially informed me that I would likely never see my computers again. I waited until the officer left. Then, I cried. Again.

I was grief-stricken. Nancy and I spent the entire day talking about being robbed and the feeling of helplessness. I should point out that our insurance company denied our claim. Apparently, because our house was under construction, we needed a special construction rider policy. We of course did not know this, but ignorance is not an excuse according to the insurance company. So there we were with essentially little hope of getting anything back and no money from the insurance company to compensate us for the loss.

But then we got down to business.

That evening, like we had done many times before in our marriage, we started to think about what we could do instead of focusing on what we couldn't control. One of the ideas that Nancy had was to offer a reward for the return of our computers.

The next day, acting on this idea, we walked into the offices of the local newspaper, the Brantford Expositor.

I had really never given it much thought, but apparently many people knew who I was. The Expositor agreed to print my story. After speaking with the reporter, he assured me that it was a good human interest story because I had played in the local theater many times and had been written up in the newspaper, as well. They figured that perhaps the publicity and the $5000 reward, which I still didn't know where that was going to come from, would prompt people to keep a lookout for my missing computer gear.

I figured that they would print a few lines in the local news section. However, when I picked up the newspaper the next day, it was right on the front page with a huge headline: "Local Jazz Musician Robbed of Life's Work."

Wow. I was floored. Obviously the story was bigger in their minds than I had anticipated. An hour later I was driving the car down West Street Hill with Nancy when I heard the news story on the radio. Again, I guess I didn't really realize the impact of this story. About 20 minutes later I received a call from someone in New Brunswick who had heard the story on their radio. Then an hour later another call came in from Vancouver. The story had made the national news wire.

This particular story seemed to have touched a nerve. I wasn't famous, but I guess when you really think about it, it is pretty tragic for a musician to lose everything that they've ever written and produced. I mean, there were two entire unreleased recorded albums on those hard drives and an entire documentary, which had also never been seen. That very same day I got a strange call from a local computer shop. They said they had something that belonged to me and that I should come down right away.

When I got there, I could see that they had one of my computers up to a monitor and had hacked the password. They told me they were about to erase the hard drive when they discovered that the information on the computer matched the story that they'd heard on the radio. Believe it or not, because the thief had pawned the computer and they had paid for it, they wanted me to pay the money that they had paid to the thief.

I know what you're thinking: Of course, I should not have to pay for my own property. I was just so happy to get it back that I gave them the $150 that they paid for it. Can you imagine paying $150 for a computer that was worth at least $2000, not to mention all the information that was on it?

One of the other computers and two other hard drives were still missing. But two days later as I was driving up to my house on Arthur Street, I could see someone sitting on the porch that I didn't recognize. Beside him sat a big brown box.

"I think I have something that belongs to you," he said as I got out of my car.

"Can I take a look?" I asked.

At that point he reached over and cracked the lid to the box slightly so that I could see inside. Sure enough, my other computer and one of the hard drives were there.

"What exactly do you want me to do now?" I asked him.

He replied, "I came for the reward."

His eyes were glazed over. Was this the thief who had broken into my house?

"Where did you get it?" I asked.

"That doesn't matter, does it?" he said.

"I'll tell you what I'm going to do." I was truly improvising at this point and piecing together phrases in my mind. I had never really been in a position to negotiate with crooks.

"I'll give you two choices. One, I'll give you whatever is in my wallet. Or two, I'll call my friend who lives one block from here and if you're still here in five minutes. You'll have to answer to both of us."

I could see that he was looking a little shaky and a little unsure about whether my threat was real or not.

It took him a second or two.

"I'll take the money," he said.

I reached into my pocket. I had $240 in there. I handed it to him and he disappeared quickly around the corner.

Think about it, though. In the end I only spent a total of $390 to recover everything except one hard drive. I never did get that one back, but I figured I was still light years ahead from where I started with nothing.

A few days later I received a call from the police.

I'm not sure to this day how it happened, but they caught the perpetrator. They gave me a mug shot to see if I knew the guy— it was the same guy who had came to my porch. They arrested him and found some of my other personal belongings in his basement. A few months later, Nancy and I gave a victim impact statement to the court and the guy got nine months in prison for possession of stolen property.

The aftermath of that event caused a bit of a stir in the Brantford community. The story was everywhere. I couldn't go anywhere in town without somebody asking me about the story and if I had gotten any of my stuff back. I must have explained it to hundreds of people over the next few years. People remember bad news— go figure.

Lesson—When Life Gives You Lemons, Juggle Them and Astound an Audience

They say that, when it comes to publicity, any news is good news. I think this story proves that. It certainly helped get my equipment back and it did create a memorable story in the minds of more people than I had ever thought possible. The experience helped propel my notoriety in the Brantford community and it undoubtedly helped people recognize me and talk about me. I didn't really mind that.

However, I didn't want to be known as the victim either, so every chance I got I would explain that the story had a happy ending.

The question that I'm trying to get you to ask yourself here is this: What is considered to be newsworthy, and how can you use that to propel your success?

You'll likely agree that most of the news you read is bad news. It's all about recounting people's misfortunes, and there is unquestionably an entertainment element to that. That may be unfortunate but it's also reality. Many people are relieved to read about other people's misfortunes because it makes them feel better about their own lives. That may seem somewhat cynical, and it is. But that doesn't make it any less real.

What I truly want you to think about is this: Has anything happened to you or your business in the past that could be considered newsworthy? There are many things you could learn about public relations and publicity that would help to propel your success. I'm not going to go into detail about all the ways that you could approach the media, but just keep it in the back of your mind—we'll get into it a bit later. Any news that happens to you or is about to happen to you, good or bad, has the potential to be a genuine help to you.

In all of the things that I have learned over the past several years that have contributed to my success, nothing is quite as powerful as this statement: "You are the company you keep."

While you may have heard that statement before, I would like to frame it in a context that could be a huge contributor to your ultimate success. What is it that rich people know that makes them different from most people? Are they all just lucky or do they have common belief systems? I have learned from experience that, indeed, rich people do think and feel differently about success than poor people. In fact one of the big differences is, while poor people want to be rich, rich people are *deeply committed* to being rich. For the most part the reasons that they choose are not completely self-serving, contrary to popular belief.

Many people believe that rich people are greedy. Really? You certainly can never become rich if you think that all rich people are greedy. It is completely contrary to the law of attraction to become something that you despise or hate. I know a lot of rich people and, in every single case, they were not greedy, but giving. In fact the ones that I know and spend time with are caring, giving, and compassionate individuals.

If all rich people were as greedy and manipulative as television makes them out to be, then who would do business with them? Don't you need to have a certain amount of integrity and build trust in order for people to do business with you? Instead of despising them many rich people should be admired for what they have accomplished.

This is a complete shift in consciousness. All you really need to do is recognize that you have built prejudices against rich people and that *this is actually keeping you from being rich*. The next time you see somebody driving a Bentley, simply say to yourself, "I respect and admire rich and successful people."

One of the first things that I did on my road to financial recovery was join the Brantford Club. Originally established in 1898 as a gentleman's social club, it has evolved over time to become the city's premiere social club. Obviously, as a private club you would expect membership fees and amenities to be expensive—that means that the people who are members are likely financially successful. I wanted to learn how rich people act, think, and feel. What better way to do it than to dive in and be among them? You might say to yourself, "I can't really afford to do that."

Well, neither could I in the beginning. But the investment was well worth it. I was becoming educated in being wealthy.

How could I afford it you ask? Well, I just made it my priority. Instead of eating out at a different restaurant every week, I would just eat at the club. Instead of spending money on movies, I would buy drinks for my friends and myself. And, in addition to being a member I offered my services as a marketer to the club to help build membership. This allowed me the opportunity to meet more people and even get some business based on those contacts. I also joined the board of directors and started a marketing committee. Then after two years of being on the board, I was asked to become vice president. I was the first artist/musician vice president of the Brantford club in their 100+-year history.

My philosophy is this: Give of yourself and expect results. I gave my time and my talents to grow the membership of the Brantford club. And, as I focused on growing the membership, my circle of influence grew and so did my number of successful friends. I never really worried about paying the bills for membership after that as the amount of business that I got by being a member and the contacts that I made far outweighed the membership fees.

Exercise—Does the Company You Keep Hold You Back?

What if I were to tell you that it is possible to double, triple or even quadruple your annual income? People do it all the time. I did, and so can you. The only difference between earning what you are earning now and earning twice as much is the knowledge and information that you could implement to get a significantly different result.

Take a moment and write down on a piece of paper how much money you will earn this year. Now, write down the amount of money that you earned five years ago. In most cases, unless you own your own business or work based on commissionable sales, your salary will be only slightly higher than it was five years ago. Based on this rate of increase how wealthy do you think you will become by squirreling away small amounts of money every year into a retirement savings plan?

Now, think about the people that you spend time with and estimate what their annual salary is. I think what you will find is that their salary is within $10,000 of your own. Based on the fact that you are the company that you keep, you will have to seek out opportunities and keep new company.

Of course, friendships are valuable in and of themselves. I am not saying get rid of your old friends. However, if you want to be wealthy then you will also have to get some new ones. Remember to never take much stock in money advice from someone in your own tax bracket. If you want to learn how to become wealthy, then you should only be taking financial advice from people in a significantly higher tax bracket.

How can you change the company you keep? Do an Internet search for a private club, a social club, or a business club in your area. You could even choose a golf club or a yacht club. Make a few phone calls and do some research on how much it would cost you per year to join one of these clubs. Then set an intention to meet with them and learn more. Remember that, when you set an intention, whatever you focus on expands, and you may find that you can afford to join the club much sooner than you thought possible.

Rich people may complain about the weather, but one of the things I've noticed is that they never complain about money. In fact, each of them has their own favourite charity and volunteer situation. People at the Brantford club were always hitting me up for money. But when it was my turn to hit them up for money for my favourite charity or event? They were always there to reciprocate. Think about it: If you tried to collect $10,000 for your charity from a local pub on a Friday afternoon, how well do you think you would do? Hah. But collecting $10,000 from people at the Brantford club seemed to be pretty easy to do. People with money are more generous than you might think. Therefore, start hanging out with people who not only spend money on the finer things in life but also on helping out their favourite charities.

Money is not an evil cancer, it is a magnifier. Having money magnifies who you are as a person. Many rich people are just as kind, compassionate, loving and giving as you are. Now imagine when you become wealthy—how much will you be able to give? And, when you give that much, how will that make you feel?

Chapter 18—Building A Millionaire Mind

One of the first friends that I made in the Brantford Club was a gentleman named Larry - a successful car dealer. He and I sat on the board together for at least four years and, in the last of those years, Larry became president. This was obviously good for me because he was such a good friend. It's always nice to have friends in high places. The day he was chosen as president, my good friend Larry presented Nancy and me with a gift. It was a book: "Secrets of the Millionaire Mind" by T. Harv Eker.

This book reconfigured how I thought about money. It was the first time I had ever heard of a "money blueprint". Your money blueprint is essentially a map of how you think and feel about money: If you feel that money is a bad thing, then you will avoid it; if you feel that money is hard to come by, then you will have to work hard for your money.

I began to realize that many of the thoughts and feelings that I had about money were adopted from a very early age and many of them were simply untrue or unhelpful. That book helped me immensely come to terms with how wealthy people think and feel. In fact, the book goes into a lot of detail about how rich people think versus poor people.

Harv's book came with two free tickets to a three-day seminar called the Millionaire Mind Intensive." In the beginning I can tell you that I was fairly skeptical about this seminar, but after discussing it with Nancy we decided to attend it in Montréal. Even if we didn't like it after the first day, at least we could visit friends and family while we were there. So, one weekend in the late spring of 2005, off we went.

My first impression upon entering that very large room at Place des Arts in downtown Montréal was one of surprise. There were more than 2000 people in that room, all on their feet dancing, clapping, and generally having a good time. And this was before the seminar even started. Initially we sat at the back just in case we wanted to make a quick exit. However, from the very first second, the speaker named Rob kept me engaged the entire time. It was enjoyable to say the least. I learned a lot about how my inner world creates my outer world. Essentially, it was a high-powered personal development seminar designed to break down your disempowering programming about money.

The thing that impressed me most about this particular seminar was the way they enrolled and engaged not only me but also thousands of people. I became intrigued with their delivery system. How were they interacting with the audience? What were some of the mechanisms that they used to keep people on the edge of their seats? I became an instant student of their delivery system. I mean, how could they get someone like me, who is generally very cool and collected, to stand up and dance, give high 5's and generally step outside my comfort zone in front of other people. This, I needed to learn.

The opportunity came to learn from them on how to do exactly what they were doing in a course called Train the Trainer. I thought to myself, *If I just take a little bit of their energy and delivery system and add it to my music career, then I might do a much better job of interacting with audiences and maybe sell more CDs*. This was my first opportunity to invest in myself (other than books). I must say that I had not anticipated how expensive it would be, but I tried to foresee results. How much would I be willing to invest if I knew I couldn't fail? I generally consider myself to be a fairly intelligent person. If they could do it, so can I. It was $3000 to take this course, plus travel expenses.

I called my dad and asked him if he would pay off one of my credit cards so that I could register for the course. This was fairly humiliating, and I obviously didn't want to do it. I also knew that it was the right thing to do. I could feel it. A few months later, in the fall of 2005, I excitedly hopped on a plane and headed to Vancouver, British Columbia to take this five-day course.

After just the first day I had the very strong feeling that my investment was going to pay off.

Two months after taking that course, I decided to put my newfound marketing and communication skills to the test. Nancy and I decided to promote a concert at the big theater in downtown Brantford. Yes, this was a huge undertaking as there are 1100 seats in that building, but, like I've said many times before, small ideas can't hold anything big. We certainly were putting a lot on the line, but how do you know if something works or not if you don't try it? This is Suggestology at its core—learning by doing.

Over 900 people showed up at that concert and I sold over 400 CDs in less than 10 minutes at intermission. With the sponsorship that I had secured from individual Brantford club members and local businesses, and with the sale of tickets and CDs, I had made my investment back from the Train the Trainer seminar in just one night!

If that's not a huge lesson in getting information from people who have what you want, I don't know what is. I mean, what better way to get information on how to run a successful event than from people who run successful events? Since that time, I spend money every year in taking seminars, webinars, and online courses from successful people. It is a great system that skips over all the trial and error and goes straight to the information that works.

One of the most valuable lessons that I took from that first Train the Trainer seminar was the concept of duty and responsibility to help others. As I've spoken about before, when you help others get what they want first, you will have what they have in abundance. If you take this statement even more seriously, then you would see it not as a choice but as a responsibility. I mean, information is supposed to be shared, isn't it? And if that is the case, then why do most businesses and most people operate based on competition and fear?

In other words, people seem to hoard information so that they can stay ahead of others. But what if the answer that you were looking for to truly achieve massive success was a change of heart?

I take this duty and responsibility very seriously, and it started all those years ago.

Now that I had some success based on a system that worked, I felt strongly about sharing it with others. Almost immediately I began to plan a seminar in Toronto based on the information that I had learned and put into practice at that concert. I quickly started a company called Success Tracks for Artists, which was all about helping musicians learn some of the things that I had learned. I wanted them to be successful from the stage, to put on their own shows, and to make a lot of money. I wanted to help others succeed.

The first seminar that I did was for approximately 20 people at the Arts and Letters Club in downtown Toronto. This seemed to be the perfect establishment not only because of its artistic heritage but because it was very inexpensive to rent the presentation hall if I became a member, which I did. When I walked into the hall, I saw something that made me grin from ear to ear—a grand piano. What better way to earn trust and credibility with an audience as a fellow artist than to play for them?

By all accounts, the training that I had received made that first seminar go pretty well. I was essentially proud of myself for diving in and taking the risk. The feedback was not particularly overwhelming, but many people there did express interest and enthusiasm for the information. However, as I had been trained to do, I made an offer for an advanced full-day course to go through all of the details that they would need to start marketing their art more aggressively and more successfully.

I did get some of the individuals to purchase a course on that first day, however, not really enough to make it profitable. . Many artists are broke and feel powerless to invest in themselves because of that lack of money. Certainly, because I had invested in myself, I really felt strongly about getting others to invest in themselves. Think about it this way: What is the point of playing poker without using real money? What do you have at risk, and what do you stand to gain, if you are not willing to invest in yourself?

No matter how much I wanted to convince these artists that their investment in a $197 full-day training was worth it, they simply couldn't see their way to part with money. One woman in particular came up to me at the end of this first seminar and said, "I love this, it's a breath in fresh air, and I have never heard anything like this in the music industry in my whole life. But, as much as I would love to take the training, I am not going to do it."

If you really want to know what someone truly means, listen only to what comes after the *but*. As I was told when I was younger, the *but* of a sentence is like the *butt* of a pencil, erasing everything that comes before it.

"Why?" I asked. "You love it. And, you know that you are going to learn something of value, so why won't you do it?"

She said, "Because I don't have any money."

"It's only $200," I replied.

She stated, "Well, I don't have $200."

I started to think about how I might reason with her and asked, "If I could sell you a house in Rosedale, the most expensive neighborhood in Toronto, for $200, would you buy it?"

She replied, "Of course."

"You can't," I replied, "You just told me that you don't have any money."

"Well, I could find money for that."

"Oh?" I smiled. "Then why wouldn't you invest $200 in yourself so that one day you could buy a real house in Rosedale?"

"If I give you the information, the structure, the template, the means to carry it out, the mindset, the laws of detachment, the laws of giving, and so on, then in all likelihood you should be able to repeat some of the successes that I have."

She shook her head. She simply wouldn't buy into my logic, and I knew right then and there that she was just the tip of the iceberg. She was one of many, a representative of most artists, and they would simply not see things my way. Sadly, I knew that Success Track for Artists was doomed to fail.

However, I continued to give these Success Tracks for Artists seminars even though there was little financial reward. It was good practice, and I knew that my intention would eventually pay off. I could have never imagined how.

One session, I began to notice that business people were starting to fill the seats of my seminars, even though the events were for artists. These were the people who owned the studios, dance companies, and even some general business owners. Most importantly, these were the people who had money. These were people who knew the importance of investing in themselves. As a result, they learned more, they grew more, and they wanted more!

I fell in love with the can-do attitude of my seminar-goers. I switched the focus of my company over to training business people and entrepreneurs. Training Business Pros was born.

Lesson—Losing the Lottery Mindset

The number one wealth-building strategy in North America is buying lottery tickets. Most people want to be wealthy; yet, most people are simply not committed to achieving wealth. The lottery is in effect the only way that most people could picture themselves becoming wealthy. It's easy.

It doesn't work, but at least it's easy. And, even on those very rare occasions when someone does when the lottery, would you be surprised to learn that 85 percent of all lottery winners return to their original state of wealth within five years? And this happens even after winning several million dollars.

Why is that?

The reason why people cannot build wealth and hold onto it is that they have had no wealth practice.

Remember the True Heart's Desire Intensity Scale? Focusing on what you want brings you closer to what you want.

In my experience, most people can tell you very easily what they do *not* want. In fact, most people would have a shopping list of gripes and complaints and situations they would die to avoid. On this shopping list would be things like too many bills and not enough money, a boss they hate, family members who cause them grief, complaints about the state of the economy, and so on.

Yet, when you finally get around to asking people what they *do* want, you tend to get very vague responses. I know because I've asked thousands of people at my seminars, and many of them don't know. You get answers like this: I don't want to be broke, or I don't want to work too hard, or I want to fear less of the unknown. If you examine the statements, these are of course structured as a sneaky way for them to just tell you what they *don't* want again.

Finally getting around to actually focusing on a goal or achieving something significant is rare. The act of learning to focus on what you want instead of what you don't is the central and integral part of the wealth building process. It is basically focusing all of your energy, or at least 85 to 90 percent of it, on what you want. It won't come immediately, but you will be given the opportunity to create it. And that is a great gift in itself.

The difference between wealthy people and poor people is the way they think. For example, a wealthy person buys a piece of cake and eats it. Their mindset says you can have cake and you eat it, too. A poor person buys a donut, focuses on the hole and wonders what is wrong with their life. Rich people leap, poor people stay put.

When you finally take that leap, you will get a result. And the great thing about results is whether they are good or bad at least you will be able to measure your results and make navigational corrections on the way to your destination. Naturally, if you attract a positive result, simply do more of the same and you will move ever closer to your goal. If you get a result that you did not expect, simply avoid it the second time around. Remember, it's only a mistake if you make it twice. Otherwise, it's a powerful learning experience.

Exercise—Practicing Wealth

Generosity is one of the key qualities of wealthy people. Certainly it's a radical concept in the minds of most people to believe that, if you want more money in your life, then you should give some away. Yet, this is *exactly* what you should be doing.

People who don't have money are afraid to give away what little they have. They don't really think about who they help by giving money away, they only think about their own personal financial situation and how it will be a little worse off if they give some of their money away. They come from a place of need, not abundance.

What you give out you will get back. This expression started as "As ye sow, so shall ye reap", which later became "You reap what you sow". But will performing good deeds actually enrich your life? Yes, it will enrich your life.

But what about monetary wealth—will hoarding your money bring that? Not likely. Unless you are generous with money, you will not see money come back to you. One of the easiest ways to practice generosity is to pick up the check for other people. When was the last time you were in a restaurant and split the check with the people at your table? Go on. Pick up the tab. I'm not asking you to do it every time, although that would be a great practice. I'm asking you to do it more than you do it now. It will feel good and others will be grateful. More than that, it is a great way to beginning to shift your mindset into one that accepts your own abundance.

Chapter 19—Keith Jarrett

About one year into the learning process, I was driving my car in the early afternoon when I heard on the radio about a famous jazz pianist named Keith Jarrett performing that evening at Roy Thomson Hall in downtown Toronto. Now this got my attention. I had studied and performed much of his music over the years. However, according to the radio announcer, it had been sold out for weeks. Initially I had thoughts of disappointment.

Then I had a thought. Can I create a different outcome that would allow me to see the sold-out concert? How can I use the law of attraction to get tickets?

I took the fact that it was a sold-out concert not as a stopping point, but as a starting point. Not as a roadblock, but as a challenge.

After reaching home, I discussed it with Nancy. We decided to go down to Roy Thomson Hall an hour in advance to see if we could purchase tickets from anyone who had extras. We knew that this was not the type of concert where there would be dozens of scalpers, but we hoped some opportunity would make itself known.

We decided to split up, figuring the odds of finding one person who's significant other didn't show up was better than trying to find one person with two tickets left over. Oh, and there was only one more thing holding us back: the cheapest ticket had been $75, and we only had a hundred between us.

We met at the doors ten minutes before show time, each with a ticket in hand. I had spent fifty on mine and Nancy had spent forty on hers, leaving us ten dollars to grab some after-concert drinks!

We kissed and agreed to meet up at the front doors after the show. I went to the bathroom and Nancy went off to her seats. Once I got out and started looking for my seats, one of the employees directed me to the eleventh row. The eleventh row for fifty dollars! I couldn't wait to tell Nancy.

And I wouldn't have to. When I got into my row, I locked eyes with Nancy. She was sitting, not only in the same row, but in the seat right beside mine. We were incredulous. Here we had great seats right behind Keith Jarrett's piano, with a perfect line of sight, and we were together.

Coincidence? You couldn't pay me to see it that way. Luck? Possibly. Law of attraction? Definitely!

Over the years I have learned to use the law of attraction to manifest everything from parking spaces to business opportunities and from great shopping deals to free stuff. I have come to expect success and because I expect it, it happens.

Lesson—Your Goals and the Law of Attraction

Activating the law of attraction requires that you not only focus on your goals, but that you focus on your *emotional guidance system*. Your feelings will guide you well if you just learn to pay close attention. If you are feeling good, you are being emotionally guided towards what you want. But as soon as you start feeling anything negative (worry, fear, doubt, and unworthiness), you are moving away from your goal. It's that simple.

Let's break it down. What triggers feeling? Your thoughts. Your thoughts trigger your feelings, which lead to the actions you take. The actions you take equal your results. If you start with negative thoughts, then you will get negative results. Dealing with your thoughts by paying attention to your feelings—your emotional guidance system—is a paramount step in reaching your goals.

Interestingly, most of the forces acting upon you that influences your thoughts and feelings come from your environment. If you or people around you keep saying, "I can't afford that," then you need to recognize that those words come from the thoughts that state the same thing. Your emotional guidance system hears these words and you feel lacking inside. It's only natural, because of your environmental programming, to feel bad when you get bad results.

Yet, when you feel bad, it is actually good, because it means your emotional guidance system is working and telling you that you are heading in the wrong direction, away from your goals. Most people resist change and avoid adopting new thoughts and feelings.

If you are unaware of the existence of your emotional guidance system then you cannot tune into it. To become aware of your emotional guidance system, lets take a specific example. Everybody deal with stress on a daily basis. But did you know that stress is a product of your emotional guidance system? Stress can be and is for many people a powerful physiological occurrence. Think about the symptoms that arise because of stress: high blood pressure, shortness of breath, sweatiness, anxiousness, and so on. Do any of those symptoms sound familiar? This is your emotional guidance system rising to the surface and letting you know that you are moving away from what you want.

Stress is the amount of energy that you put into resisting your situation. The more energy you put into resisting your situation, the more your situation will persist. Pay attention to the symptoms of stress and use them as a compass to signal a change in direction from what you don't want to what you do want.

Once you become aware of the symptoms of stress, you can take steps to change your direction. The fact that you are stressed means that you are resisting. Once you realize this shift, your focus moves to acceptance. This is the least amount of energy that you will need to start moving you in a more positive direction. It is certainly not the most powerful form of energy, but it's a good start!

Now, be careful how you define acceptance. Most people would define acceptance as putting up with the things that they don't want. That is not acceptance at all! In fact if you really examine it, putting up with the things that you don't want is *resistance*.

Acceptance means that you are truly fine with whatever situation is confronting you. You are at peace no matter what forces are acting upon you. You also know that this is not where you want to be. Therefore, you have a quiet expectation that things are about to change or get better. There is nothing wrong with expecting better. Most people expect the worst and hope for the best. Not you, though. From now on, you expect the best and know that where you are is a good starting point. You are in acceptance of the way things are. For most people this is a very radical concept, yet once you get good at it, you will begin to see that things can change rapidly. Grow into acceptance. Nothing will ever change if you continue to resist.

In simpler terms, let's think of an example with which you may be able to relate: Imagine you are working a dead-end job, and your boss is a real piece of work. The idea of accepting your position in the company and that your boss has issues is not the same as *saying your circumstances are okay with you.* You accept the reality of the situation, you realize that you are better off living in a reality than trying to deny it, and then you use that reality as fuel to excite and propel you into a new position of employment—or management yourself!

Once you go inside yourself and use your emotional guidance system it will tell you that acceptance is the first solution. You will then have a quiet expectation that things will get better and, once you focus on things getting better, they will.

When I was first learning about the law of attraction, I found it very difficult because that is not the way that I was taught. I compare it to navigating the ocean at night. There's no point of reference and no solid GPS. All I had to do was learn to trust my emotional guidance system. Then, little by little I started to see results. There were small indications that if I could control my thoughts then I could start to attract the very things I desired.

Exercise—Use the Flip Switch

The first time I ever heard of the *flip switch* was from Dr. Robert Anthony, in his audio series entitled "The Secret Of Deliberate Creation". Essentially, the flip switch is a metaphor for shifting your focus from negative thoughts to positive ones. The more positive the thought, the greater the magnetic attraction. Thoughts are magnetic and draw to them like energy. This is the essence of the law of attraction.

Obviously, for the flip switch to work, you must be constantly monitoring your emotional guidance system. When you feel bad, it is the perfect opportunity to use the flip switch. Let's try it now. Think of something right now that is bothering you. Paint a mental picture of the situation that you do not like. Feel the negativity associated with that situation. It could be financial problems, relationship problems, or even something that happened at work today. No matter what the situation, make sure that it is something that makes you feel bad.

You're probably wondering why I want you to feel bad. I don't, but I do need you to be aware of how the exercise actually works so go ahead and feel bad for just a moment.

Now that you have pictured in your mind the negative situation, I want you to imagine that there is a light switch on the back of your neck. It is currently set in the *off* position. Since the light is off it is a dark place, a negative place, a place that makes you feel bad. All you have to do now is reach around your right hand and flip the switch to the *on* position and say the following words out loud: "I choose to feel happy now."

As you say these words imagine white light all around you as a result of turning on the switch on. Situations and circumstances do not make you feel bad; only you can do that. Situations themselves mean nothing unless you associate meaning with them.

When you feel better and happier you will begin to attract, like a magnet, new situations and circumstances that will be associated with the positive magnetic vibrations that you put out. Like attracts like. This is an irrefutable law of the universe.

It is such a simple thing to do that perhaps you think it will not work. The only reason it will not work if you don't try it. Try it now if you haven't already.

In my experience, these are possibly the six most powerful words that you will ever say to yourself.

"I choose to feel happy now."

When you learn to say these words to yourself, you will be forming new, more positive habits in your life. Your focus will change from what is wrong in your life and you will begin to focus more on what is possible.

If you are to ever attract the life that you desire, you will most certainly have to adopt more empowering habits. The flip switch is one of those habits that you will have to practice. The act of reaching around with your hand and turning on the flip switch and saying those six powerful words may seem like a small thing. But I can assure you that it is a very powerful exercise. Believe it first, and then you will see the manifestations of it. Seeing is not always believing.

Chapter 20—When Worlds Collide

More and more each day my life was evolving further away from music and drawing closer to a life of training and speaking. As I look back on it now, I can honestly say that I became an *accidental trainer*, meaning that I kind of fell into it. The training that I had received made it very clear that I had a duty and responsibility to help others achieve greater success in their lives.

I took this very seriously. So even though most of my life had been spent pursuing a career in music, I began to love speaking and training. It felt as if I was meant to help others, and I began to groove with it just as much as I could hold a groove in music. People still ask me if I miss the music business and of course I do, but I can go back to it whenever I want and not feel the horrible weight of having to make a living with it.

The Brantford Club was a big part of my life at this point. Nancy and I would often go there for lunch. Every Friday night, being members' night, you would find us right in the middle of the action. We started to develop some great friends and even some new business relationships. The Board of Directors would meet once a month over lunch and discuss the ongoing business of the club. Aside from the usual discussions of building maintenance, finances, and human resources, we began to have heated discussion about attracting new members. Membership is the lifeblood of any organization. Several ideas were thrown around about how to attract new members and while many of them were okay, we couldn't decide on the best course of action.

I had been vice president for a while and even though I was a fairly new member compared to the rest of the board, people seemed to listen to what I had to say when it came to marketing. So, I spoke up and said, "Why don't we have an open house?"

The room became silent, so I continued, "You know, we could invite people from the community to come to a special evening at the club and it wouldn't even cost us anything. Why not? Because, there will be entertainment and I am certain that people would pay for the entertainment. Once we have that captive audience, we could make a special offer to them concerning membership. For example, we could waive their initiation fees and reduce their first six months membership dues. Or we could lower the initiation fees and forgive membership dues for six months, or something like that."

"That's a great idea," Larry, the club president, said. "What kind of entertainment were you thinking of?"

"Well, I think it should be someone with a bit of a name, someone who is well-known in the community and who could attract a full house. It should also be entertainment fitting with the class and style of the Brantford club." Everyone hesitated uncomfortably because they knew what was coming, as if I had set it up that way, which I did. "How about me?"

It was a bold offer to be sure, and more than a little self-serving, but hey, if you don't ask, you don't get.

"There is only one problem," Larry said. "We don't have a piano."

"No problem, I'll donate mine. All we need to do is hire a moving company and tune it. No big deal. I'll even use my own personal mailing list to invite the people who I think should become members of the club, and each of you will be responsible to bring at least two potential members to the concert and dinner."

While there was some resistance on the behalf of some of the board members, the idea was voted upon and passed. Next thing

I knew, I became the entire marketing team and flag waver for this event. There was a lot at stake, and I knew that if I couldn't fill the room with potential members then the whole purpose of the open house would fail. So I stepped into it with everything that I had and it worked.

We filled the club to capacity and every available seat in the dining room was occupied and then some. The piano was moved upstairs into the largest available room and we set up theater seating wall-to-wall.

After dinner, everyone made their way up the stairs to the performance room. My two worlds were colliding as not only did I have the responsibility of performing but I also have the responsibility of selling membership.

I began by using my bulletproof introduction template and immediately took control of the room in the direction of the energy. With the combination of well-known jazz standards, popular music, and choice stories, the evening became electric.

Then, as I had planned beforehand, I introduced the song, *Green Green Grass Of Home.* How I did it and the version of that song that I played was the absolute hit of the evening as it drew together important club members in the story. Please take a moment right now and go to the Internet and download the introduction and the recording of the song. I really want you to get a feel for how my worlds were colliding so that you can begin to bring together the most exciting parts of your life.

http://www.trainingbusinesspros.com/m/green-green-grass

Music is my first love, yet I was learning that there were many things that I could enjoy in life besides music. Perhaps you have been missing things that you love to do. Maybe you could use this story as inspiration to get back to the things that you love and combine them with a purpose and a message.

Lesson—Enjoying What You Do and Beyond!

Positive energy is more than simply accepting, although that is a good place to start. If you are vibrating with emotions stronger than just "acceptance", then you are going to attract what you want even faster. As you know by now—the stronger the energy, the stronger the attraction.

As we've discussed, your emotional guidance system leads you to success. As you choose to grow and use your positive energy, you will find that you are enjoying yourself. And rightly you should! Yes, there will be roadblocks. However, as a hurdler understands that the hurdles are all part of the game, you understand that challenges are just part of life, and move past them with negligible effort.

When you increase your positive energy to the level of enjoyment, your attraction is magnetic. This is called Creative Magnetic Energy. Any energy that you put into getting what you want will take a certain amount of creativity. This kind of energy draws situations, circumstances, and people towards you. When you love what you do, you will be enjoying life. Enjoyment broadcasts to everyone around you that you love what you do. It is not complicated to see why this draws people to you.

Everyone has something they love to do. We may not do it a lot, but we still love it. For example, nobody needs to tell me to go play golf. I find the time to golf because I want to. I'm not the greatest golfer on the planet, but I love it.

What do you love to do?

Show me something that you love, and I will show you someone who makes money doing it. You do not need to be a professional golfer to make money in golf; almost none of the people who make money in golf are. You could start a golf business, coach or teach golf, run a golf club, or even build a golf course. There are endless ways to get what you want.

Beyond acceptance and enjoyment is yet another higher level. It's the highest level of energy that you could emit. It is called *enthusiasm*. When you are enthusiastic about something, there is no stopping you. Why? Because you simply won't be denied! You cannot be stopped; the universe bends to your will. You see potential problems as useful components that will help inform your decisions. Enthusiasm is infectious and will draw people to you. You will be magnetized at the highest level possible.

The great thing about enthusiasm is there's actually a formula to create it. It's simple: Enjoyment + Goal = Enthusiasm

Simply put, love what you do and create a big goal around it. If you love to help people, create a business around helping people. You could become a life coach or a motivational speaker. If you love fixing cars, start a garage business, and one day maybe even fix Formula One cars.

Create a visual picture and feeling in your mind and in your heart. Every day, practice that feeling. Start your day with that. Most people wake up, watch the news (it's all bad), then at night they watch the news again (it's still all bad), and so they start and end the days with bad news. Do you, too?

Try not to start your day by listening to the news and hearing about other people's misfortunes. Focus on what you want instead. The first thought of your day should be, "What is my ultimate destination?"

I awake almost every day with that destination in my head. It used to be hard to remember, but, with practice and time, it became easier, and results came quicker.

Exercise—Keep Going

Acknowledge your gifts

You cannot change what you do not acknowledge. To that end you must monitor the energy of your thoughts and feelings. One of the most critical times of the day to begin to monitor your thoughts and feelings is first thing as you wake up.

Have you ever noticed that there is a period of calm between sleep and consciousness? As you awaken into conscious thoughts, are you immediately drawn to negativity? It may be a challenge from the previous day or the anticipation of a problem in the future.

If you are not used to waking up with positively charged energy, then begin by reading or listening to a book or CD by somebody who speaks a language that feels good. If you are drawn to any particular writer or speaker, you are heading in the right direction, no matter what anybody else says. Start your day with 10 minutes of that positively charged message. Then repeat the same thing at the end of the day.

What will happen if you do this? A habit will form. Eventually you will wake up to abundance and fall asleep to happiness. Eventually the vast majority of your day will be filled with enthusiasm and positively charged thoughts and feelings.

Pick Your Healing Spot

Next, find a location in your house that you pass by several times a day. Each time you pass by this spot, remember to speak a few well-chosen positive words to yourself. The words that you choose are not as important as simply learning to say them.

For example, I used to have a landing in my old house between the second and third floors. I'm speaking of the house where we had to repair the foundation. Over time, we transformed that house into a beautiful home, and on the third floor we created an office space where I could start my new business. We added skylights, beautiful plank floors, and motivating colors and lighting. As I headed up to the third floor, several times a day, I would reach that landing between the second and third floor and say to myself two very simple words:

"Keep going!"

I first learned those words while walking across Spain. No matter what pain that I was feeling in my legs, ankles, knees, or back, I repeated those words whenever I needed to hear them. As I built my business and ran into challenges and roadblocks, I always had the time to, as I reached that landing between the second and third floors, encourage myself to keep going.

Take a moment and think about a place that you pass by every day. It could be a doorway, a table, a desk, or even your own stairs or landing area. Think about the words that you would choose to motivate yourself to keep going. Maybe the words for you are "Keep going", as well. It doesn't need to be. Any words will do as long as they keep you motivated to move forward towards your goals.

When you feel bad or feel resistance you are moving away from what you want. Simply switch your focus back onto what you want and be in the process of creating it.

How will you know when you are moving towards your goals? When you feel good. Your emotional guidance system will keep you on track.

Chapter 21—Advanced Piano Lessons

Despite shifting paradigms on what it means to be "retired", advertising and other pressures have been telling the common person to save for what they say is an inevitable milestone of later life. Retirement savings plans are constantly being touted by big banks as an effective way to put money away on a regular basis and earn enough interest so that when you retire you will have enough to live your current lifestyle. However, for the most part you will likely have to cut back on your lifestyle when you retire.

I do believe that, while you should certainly make sure there is money left over for you for your twilight years, you also need to know that there are alternatives to squirreling money away at a negligible interest rate.

One of the ways that I have learned to create a steady stream of income without having to work is to create intellectual property that has market value. There are many types of intellectual property ranging from products that entertain people to products that inspire and educate. Some examples of intellectual property that you could create are books, e-books, videos, smart phone and tablet apps, CDs, software, membership websites, etc. Intellectual property is valuable in whatever form it comes in as long as it can give value to another person or a business.

However, you must know what you're doing. You must create it for other people. In other words, it must have market appeal. I wrote music for, arranged, recorded and produced eight jazz music CDs. Because of the tight niche jazz market, these CDs had limited appeal. For one thing, I am not a famous jazz musician. Typically, jazz musicians who have been dead for many years sold more CDs in a day than I sold in a year. For example, musicians like Thelonious Monk, Charlie Parker, and

John Coltrane are typically gargantuan in the jazz market. Naturally, in order to sell as many CDs as them, I would have to become famous. The likelihood of that actually happening seemed to me to be incredibly remote. So remote, in fact, that I actually walked away from the music industry.

How can I make money through intellectual property if people do not want to buy my CDs? One of the things that occurred to me was I don't actually have to think of it myself; I have to find out what I can give that other people want.

However obvious this may seem, it was a radical thought for me. That you don't actually have to think up anything new, that all you have to do is ask people what they would be willing to pay for? It was an exciting prospect. That's exactly what I did.

I had been building websites for a very long time because, of course, I couldn't really afford to hire anyone else to do it. A natural progression of this skill set would be to learn marketing and make my websites more attractive to the general public. I wasn't really interested in this until the Closer To The Dream project, which I mentioned in chapter 15.

When I met Tony, as a result of that project, I was introduced to a whole new world of marketing. I started learning that it's not what you sell that matters but how you sell it. One of the most important lessons that I learned in selling?

"The money's in the list."

This simply means that you create a targeted mailing list of subscribers by giving them free valuable content in exchange for their contact information. Once you have that contact information, you can introduce them to new products or services simply by e-mailing them, or ask them what they'd like to see from you.

This is a form of Suggestology. When you ask people what they want, you are poking their attention and getting them to zero in on their creativity.

I decided to employ a couple of key marketing concepts in one. I would use the concept of search engine optimization to drive traffic to a single webpage and then collect the visitor e-mail addresses in exchange for something of value. What was the value that I decided to offer them? There were many things that I could offer, but I decided simply to offer them a discount on an upcoming information product. I simply created a headline to hook the visitors' interest in that headline read as follows:

Advanced Online Video Piano Lessons By Concert Jazz Pianist Paul Tobey.

Learn To Improvise Using Accelerated Learning Methods That Will Help You Learn Faster and Retain More

COMING SOON

Register here to save 50% and have the opportunity to give feedback on what you would like to see incorporated into these advanced level video piano lessons.

First Name [   ]

Email   [   ]

I really didn't do much more than that, except give some ideas on what I thought should be included in this video series.

Are you getting any ideas yet? Think about it. All you really have to do is build a webpage and build a mailing list based on something that you intend to do and not something that you've actually done yet. Many people make the mistake of building something first by spending a lot of money on research and development. Then, by the time the product is ready, they are out of money. Marketing for most people comes last. For me, it comes first. It's a radical concept: market first—deliver later.

And that's exactly what I did with my video piano lessons. Before creating a course I simply threw up this webpage that promised people a discount once the product was ready. It gave me the opportunity to ask them what type of information they feel would provide value to them. It semi-personalized the online content they were paying for. They had a helping hand in its creation. Sure, I can make an educated guess at what I think is good content, but what is the harm in asking other people what they want?

Before I knew it, 500 people joined the list. Five hundred! It turned out that this particular product is something that people really wanted. It costs a lot of money to take private lessons and usually you will not get those lessons with a professional musician without spending a lot of money. And, I received e-mails from dozens of people requesting to incorporate information about improvise additional techniques, jazz harmony, blues, scales, practice techniques and more.

When it came time to spend some money and actually make the videos, I was armed powerful information. And it was going to cost a lot of money. How much do think it would cost to hire a film crew, build a set, move the piano, tune the piano, film for four days, take hundreds of hours of footage from several cameras, and edit that into one 10-part video series? In the end, more than $20,000. Yes, that's a lot of money. But what you should also know is that, by the time we were done filming and editing, there were now 3,300 people on the list. Wow!

It took several months to finish and that entire time my webpage was collecting customer data. Then one Friday evening before leaving with Nancy to do a three-day seminar with Tony Robbins, I sent out a personalized e-mail to all 3,300 people at once, using auto responder software. That e-mail went something like this:

Hi John,

Are you ready to get started taking your piano skills to the next level?

You preregistered to receive a 50% discount on my "advanced online video piano lessons course." Well, the course is now ready and you are one of the first to hear about it.

Click here now to read how you can get the entire 10 video piano lessons at 50% off and some incredible sheet music bonuses just for waiting so long.

Enjoy the course,

Paul Tobey

P.S. Please forward this e-mail to any friend or family member or colleague who could also benefit and I'll give them the discount as well. Thank you.

I clicked send on the e-mail, got in the car, and drove away.

The entire weekend my BlackBerry would buzz in silent mode about every five or ten minutes. The 50% discount on the course made the actual sale price $247. By the end of the weekend I had made my entire investment back. All with one e-mail. Since then, because the piano lessons are digitally downloadable, my cost is pretty much zero. (All I have to do is pay for web hosting.)

Every time someone buys these lessons from me, it is almost all profit. One of the things that I know about this particular course is that the information will never go out of style. Playing the piano is a very specific skill and, while the delivery method for the information may change, learning how to play jazz piano won't. Now that's a retirement plan you can take to the bank— just not literally!

Lesson—Intellectual Property

What are you knowledgeable about?

What have you learned in your life and succeeded at that other people might not know how to do?

What challenges have you overcome?

What are you passionate about?

Do you have a message to share with other people?

Do you have a unique story to share?

You could lead, teach, and inspire the world with the wealth of knowledge you've accrued over your lifetime. You may not think it, but it's true. And not only can you help others, but you can help others while making residual income and turning a profit off of the knowledge you've amassed over the years. What goes around comes around, and, by endeavouring to help others, the universe will drop rewards to you. However, it may not be at your doorstep: It may be in your front porch, or back door, or down your chimney, or in the attic. Don't look for financial gain or reward in the very place that you think it will come from, standing on your front step with your arms crossed. Yes, you could simply sell your information and get paid. Yet, that's not the only reward that you will see. That's the part that many people don't see. The reason why most people would never attempt something like this is because they believe that their information is less worthy than others. Did you shy away when you read up there that you could lead, teach, and inspire the world?

Whatever your self-perceived limitations are, the fact is that your information is valuable to *someone*. And, whether you sell it or give it away for free, it's still going to bring you some type of reward. Usually, that reward is more opportunity. Sometimes, though, it's monetary.

Here's an interesting statistic to consider: Did you know that if you make more than $2750 a year, then you earn more money than 85 percent of the population living on this planet? Did you know that if you make more than $27,500 a year, then you are in the top 10 percent of the wealthiest people on planet Earth?

What does that mean for you?

That means there are a lot of people on planet Earth who have not seen the success that you have. That is your opportunity to help them.   Millions. The internet has shrunk the planet considerably. All you have to do is learn some simple marketing skills to get your information out.

Essentially your mission, should you choose to accept it, is to create marketing material that enrols and engages people, getting them to take action by joining your mailing list. Then, simply poll your audience and ask them what they want. Obviously, you will want to target your niche audience. If you find an audience that is currently being underserviced, then you could become quite wealthy by building a steady stream of residual income as an *infopreneur*.

Exercise—Begin With A Marketing Plan

Challenge yourself to come up with a marketing plan to sell information products. Some of the things that you would want to consider in your marketing plan are as follows:

Who is your target audience?

Is this market currently being serviced? If so, by whom?

How can you learn more about internet marketing best practices?

What is the form that your e-learning product would take?

Do you know anyone who could help you?

There is much to learn about marketing and the best way to get your information products into the hands of other people. One of the most effective things that you could ever do to create residual income based on intellectual property is register for training courses from someone who has the skill set and knowledge you desire. Somebody who's been where you've been, and done what you want to do.

My company, Training Business Pros, has several hundred hours of online training courses and a steady stream of live seminars throughout the year that teaches internet marketing, various sales skills, presentation courses and even courses on how to create intellectual property that sells.

I encourage you to do some research on our website. Better yet, go to this URL and sign up for Tobeyisms. In this free video newsletter, I share the latest tips and tricks on what's new and what's not in marketing.

http://www.trainingbusinesspros.com/m/tobeyisms

Chapter 22—Bayview Village

As I was evolving steadily away from the old paradigm—constant worry, fear and resistance— to a new one—becoming a deliberate creator, opportunities, trusting the universe—more opportunities came my way. I was forging strong relationships at the Brantford Club and became a well-known fixture as the club's vice president. The natural progression is from vice president to president, and it soon became my time to take the presidency. Whether I felt worthy of this position or not, it became clear to me that, were it my duty and responsibility to do so, I would simply have to do it. I had some idea of the time commitment that comes with the duties of being the president—perhaps more than I was prepared for, but the club had been very good to me, and I felt strongly about serving as president.

Tradition states that an election be held, but it is largely a formality because of the natural order of a group so steeped in tradition. Or so I thought. As it turned out, a movement was afoot to make sure that in the 125-year history of the Brantford club, no artist or musician would ever be given the role of president. At the very last minute, literally, another member was nominated to run against me as president.

I had many friends at this time, all of who were looking out for my best interest. Friend after friend came to me at the club in private or called me on the phone to let me know of the campaign to oust me from the board itself. Most people, when put in this position, would fight back with force. Everyone else wanted me to fight.

I looked at it like this: If the membership felt strongly that a musician should not be president, then who was I to fight them on it? Quite frankly, I wasn't sure I wanted to take on all of the responsibilities of president. So, contrary to what everyone else wanted me to do, I stayed silent, and I ended up losing the election.

As a deliberate creator, I knew that whenever a door closes, a window opens. It was only a matter of time before I would see evidence in my physical reality that what had happened at the Brantford club was to propel me forward. Good friends felt bad for me and let me know in no uncertain terms that they did not support the other president or the tactics that were used to oust me. However I assured them that I did not take it personally.

In fact, I was grateful for the outcome, for what happened next was to solidify my purpose as well as drive me towards another city of opportunity—Toronto.

I had been traveling back and forth to Toronto at least four times a week for several months. This ate up three hours of my day. Plus, it made it very difficult to schedule meetings and run seminars. Business was heating up and more people were coming to my presentations. It was clear to me that it was time to make the move. Not being elected as the president of the Brantford club was just the sign I needed to get my butt in gear and follow the breadcrumbs to success.

The only challenge? Money. Toronto is a completely different real estate market with even the most modest of homes commanding resale values in excess of $600,000. However, how would it appear to seminar participants and business associates for me to be living in that level of housing?

I know what you're thinking! But contrary to what you may assume, my vanity has did not enter into this concern. It's simply a matter of how business people are perceived by other business people. In business you must walk your walk, and not just talk the talk. And even though I was sitting on close to $500,000 in property in Brantford Ontario, the switch to the Toronto market would take every ounce of courage I had, and some help from the universe, to come up with the money needed.

Nancy and I started looking at property in Toronto. With a population of 2.5 million people and another 5 million in the GTA (Greater Toronto Area), Toronto is a mecca for business people and high-level talent. I knew that I was ready, however, the real estate discrepancies between Brantford in Toronto were fast. The Brantford market at this time was extremely soft. I listed both my properties, my personal residence, and the rental property that I owned, but the real estate agent let me know in no uncertain terms that it would likely take some time to get anywhere close to my asking price. I of course needed my price to make the leap to the much higher priced real estate in Toronto.

With my house listed, Nancy and I made frequent trips to Toronto to work with Barbara, who was the real estate agent of good friends. It was not easy. We looked for several months. It became evident that even $900,000 wasn't going to be enough.

It looked bad, but I knew in my heart that something would happen. Deliberate creators always know this. I trusted the process and just kept going. I don't know how many houses we visited, but it was a lot, and nothing spoke to me. I could tell that Barbara was getting frustrated with the process and just kept telling me to take a leap of faith and pick something. I'm all for taking a leap of faith, but I don't want to move into a house that doesn't speak to me. I refused to settle. I know enough about real estate and have owned enough property to make the calculation in my head between value and feeling good about your physical surroundings. I had always taken pride in my properties. I have learned, from reading several books and listening to audio CDs by Dr. Dolf De Roos, how to make a property more valuable than when I purchased it so that the resale value could make me some tax-free income.

Deliberate creators know that there is a perfect time to take action. Logic and reason in most cases have very little to do with the decision-making process of deliberate creators. You go with how you feel. I simply put in a request in my "ESP request box" to deliver me the perfect property and took action towards finding it. It wasn't really that much effort, as Nancy and I were enjoying our trips to Toronto and the house-hunting process. We were of course a little scared because of the big money risks, but I kept assuring Nancy that the money would come. I was thinking to myself that just being in Toronto would allow me more time to connect with people and more opportunity to build my reputation as well as my speaking and marketing business.

Summertime came and we still had not found a property. We decided to rent a cottage for a month in the village of Niagara-on-the-Lake. This is a popular tourist destination on the weekends, but a sleepy little town during weekdays. We found a quaint little cottage and put my son Adrian in sailing school at the local yacht club.

About two weeks into our vacation, I received a call from Barbara. I had let her know in no uncertain terms that if anything came up in terms of available properties I would be willing to make the trip to Toronto on short notice. She was particularly excited about a property in Bayview village, and she made it clear to me that it required urgent attention. The Toronto market is such that when a property of value comes on the marketplace in a hot community like Bayview village, you do not wait around a couple of days. Twenty minutes later I was in the car heading to Toronto. Nancy could not come because she had prior commitments, and so I made the trip myself.

When I pulled up in the driveway of this beautiful home in Bayview and got out of my car to greet Barbara, I knew that this was the one. She had told me on the phone what the asking price was and I kept thinking during the entire trip to Toronto how crazy it was to even bother showing up. Asking price: 1.3 million. How is it even possible for a jazz musician who just bought a home two years earlier for $125,000, to even consider such a move?

That's where the deliberate creator part comes in. Jump in and figure things out later. If it feels right and it's meant to be, somehow a deliberate creator will make it happen.

So, with a sense of excitement and hesitancy, I entered what I knew would soon become my home with Barbara. My jaw dropped. The home was approximately five years old and custom-built to perfection. It showed some signs of wear, but I looked beyond that to the vaulted ceilings, winding staircases, six bedrooms, six bathrooms, custom kitchen, open-space living, and the perfect bay window for my grand piano.

"I'll take it!" I proclaimed loudly after just 20 minutes of exploration throughout the three levels.

"How can we make this happen?" I asked. I had told Barbara that our maximum budget was $900,000, and even then we weren't sure that the bank would allow it. "There's a big difference between nine hundred thousand and one point three million," I told her.

"You let me worry about that," she said with confidence. "I know the real estate agent personally. We've done business before, and he owes me one," said Barbara, flashing me a devilish grin.

I knew she was a smart cookie and would probably get the price down. I called Nancy in Niagara-on-the-Lake and told her the situation. I told her I found the perfect house and that we needed to put down an offer that instant.

Nancy was hesitant, but trusted my intuition and expertise. We went for it.

I know what you're thinking and yes, we still owned our properties in Brantford, which had not sold and would likely not sell for some time. Would the equity in those houses be enough for the bank to allow us to purchase a million-dollar home? That of course was the question on my mind.

Miraculously, because the house was not being lived in at the time, and because of the financial situation of the vendor and the relationship between Barbara and the real estate agent, we managed to come to an agreement of $1.13 million, quite a bit less than the actual asking price. This was literally unheard of in the Toronto marketplace even though the entire economy was going through recession.

Twenty-four hours later I received a call from Martin at the bank.

"Here's the deal," he started. "I can get you nine hundred thousand. You'll have to come up with the balance in cash."

Uh oh, I thought as my energy shifted from excited to worry. *Where am I going to come up with $230,000 in cash?* My houses hadn't sold. This was going to be very difficult, and I only had four days to come up with the money. The price was right, the house felt right, and even though the timing wasn't perfect at first glance, timing is always perfect in the mind of a deliberate creator.

In the end, we came up short by just $60,000. So close, yet so far. Where could we possibly get $60,000 in cash? We had tapped out all our credit and pulled in every single favour we could think of from everyone we could think of. That's when Nancy got one of her famous bright ideas.

You see, Nancy has crankshaft Angels. What are crankshaft Angels? She managed to find a crankshaft for a 1984 Suzuki GS 1150 when no one else could. Does she know anything about motorcycles? No, but she made that happen, and it happened in the most unlikely of places. Ever since that time early in our marriage she was known to have crankshaft Angels.

She said, "What if we went to the vendor himself and asked him to front us the sixty thousand for two months until we can figure out a way to come up with it ourselves?" Great idea. She ran it by the real estate agent Barbara, who agreed to call the vendor with the proposal.

Long story short? The vendor agreed. We had just bought ourselves a $1.3 million home. Unbelievable.

Almost overnight, we were heading into a new era of wealth. It felt good. No, it felt great.

As a footnote to this story, and as I write this chapter, you need to know that the property around us in Bayview village has gone up considerably in value and the same home that we purchased for $1.13 million is now valued, based on a recent re-evaluation, at over $2 million in just two and a half years. How's that for making the right decision?

Lesson—Introducing Your ESP

Most people, when they think ESP, think Extra Sensory Perception. I, on the other hand, would like to introduce to you the notion of an "essential silent partner," a term that I've learned from Dr. Robert Anthony.

What is your essential silent partner? This is your higher self. Some people call it the soul, and others call it your essence of being. It is the part of you that knows everything about you as well as everything you do not, such as where you came from and where you're going. It has the answers you need and the guidance systems to get you where you want to go. Think of your ESP as the person you would want to be if you were a perfect being. Your ESP has a direct connection to source energy. Even though you may have lost that connection and are missing the language of communication to connect, your ESP still knows it: always has and always will. Your essential silent partner can be spoken to and connected with if you just know how to do it. If you want something, then all you have to do is ask your ESP, put in a request, and wait for that request to be fulfilled. It sounds simple, and it is. Anyone who doubts the effectiveness of any essential silent partner is likely right. Yet, you cannot always be right and still get what you want. What if your essential silent partner is real and all you need to do is test the connection?

A conversation and a connection between you and your essential silent partner goes beyond logic and reason. The mind cannot fathom this type of relationship. The mind is insignificant in comparison to the vast array of spiritual knowledge that your ESP holds. The mind will doubt and resist the connection. Do not allow this. When you turn decisions over to your ESP and wait for things to be delivered to you, you are then communicating with a higher level of consciousness.

Situations and circumstances are drawn to you based on your energy. If your energy is in resistance, then you will draw to you negative energy and negative circumstances. Communicating with your ESP allows you to vibrate on a higher level of consciousness and draw higher forms of energy to you. What you draw to you is opportunity to discover your power as a deliberate creator.

Please go through the exercise section of this chapter carefully and follow the directions as laid out. If you doubt, that is okay. All you have to do is carry out the instructions and manifest your desires. Let the manifestation of these desires become the proof you need to believe your ESP is real and that your connection to your higher self is the most powerful connection you can make on planet Earth. Your partner is silent yet essential to your powers of manifestation. Becoming a deliberate creator will require you to keep an open channel to your ESP and learn through practice how to communicate with it. One day you, too, will be able to manifest whatever you desire.

Exercise—Communicating With Your ESP

Set up an ESP request box.

This is a fun and effective way to deliberately create and manifest anything you desire. Basically the idea is to put in a request just like you would make an order at a restaurant. You can request anything you like—from small goals to big ones, interim desires to ultimate desires. Exactly how those desires manifest in your life is not the concern of this exercise. Simply put in the request and wait for it to come to you.

Remember that you must always take action in the direction of your desires, but how they manifest and what direction they take is up to your ESP. In other words, turn things over to your ESP and let him or her handle the details.

Any box will do for your ESP request box. Make it or buy it. Make use of a family heirloom or use a cigar box. It could be made of plastic, wood or even metal. Decorate it or don't. No one box is better than another. Just make it is unique to you and then put it in a place where others cannot disturb it. You do not want others to interfere with your communication process.

Once you have chosen a special place to keep it, put it in its place and say the following out loud: "This is my special ESP request box. From now on, when I put a request in this box, I ask you my essential silent partner, to act on my request immediately. I thank you in advance for your response to my requests."

Write out your requests on a piece of paper and stick them in the box. Do them one at a time. There is no special way to write out your requests, but here is an example of the way that I write my own requests:

Dear ESP,

I request a big white yacht with two state rooms and plenty of space to entertain friends, family, and colleagues. This or something better.

I thank you in advance for your response to this request.

Sincerely,

Paul Tobey

Finally, place the request in your ESP request box and say a quick mantra: something like "Thank you ESP, in advance, for your response to my request."

When you take focused action on this level, it activates the law of attraction and encourages your essential silent partner to bring your requests to you. Your focus is everything, and this exercise will keep you *focused.*

I am as logical and reasoning as the next person, but part of that is knowing the limits of one's own understanding. One thing I can say with the utmost certainty about this exercise is this: If you do not do it, it will most certainly not work.

Take a look at your current results and ask yourself, "Do my results reflect the efficiency of a great system?" If not, try this exercise. What do you have to lose? Many people would think that, because of the simplicity of this system, it couldn't possibly work. Those same people would say that it's simply not realistic. To them I respond with, you guessed it, "Reality is for people who lack imagination."

In fact, Stephen Covey, the late famous bestselling author of "The Seven Habits of Highly Successful People" said, "Live out of your imagination, not your history." What he's really saying is that your history is likely made up of a series of misfortunes and small successes. If that is all you have to rely on to create your future, then you are very limited in what you will be able to do because your history will tell you that it's impossible. That is why you must learn to connect with your essential silent partner. Your creations depend on it.

Not everything in your reality is created by hard work and reasoning. Many of the things that you own or have accomplished in your life are a result of you either having a strong connection with your ESP or no connection at all. Usually what I find with people who do not have a strong connection with their ESP is that they live life by default. Most people who are not deliberate creators live life through a series of problems. Is this any way to live?

Do not put any time restrictions or limitations on the results that you manifest as a result of a connection with your essential silent partner. The mind will want to control the situation, but the mind cannot grasp this connection. Only the heart can understand what is truly happening here. If it feels good, then you are heading in the direction of your goals. Doing the ESP exercise is one way to feel good and a very powerful way to bring about monumental change.

Incidentally, my request for the big white yacht has been fulfilled, not to mention dozens of other requests. I believe in it because I had seen firsthand that my essential silent partner is real and I trust in him to deliver me a steady stream of requests. He and I together are dedicated and efficient deliberate creators.

Chapter 23—Leadership

Most if not all of the life that you want to create for yourself is dependent, as I have stated before, on how great you become at deliberately creating it. Part of that process is not only the inner strength that you rely on to keep you going but also on how others perceive you. In my experience one of the most important elements to creating financial wealth in your life is not only for you to believe in yourself but for others to believe in you, too, and for them to want a piece of what you have created.

I'm talking about leadership. It is very difficult for people to believe in followers. If you cannot create the perception of leadership then it will be difficult, if not impossible, for others to give you money for your products and services, pay you for your expertise, invest in you, or even support you.

The reality is that people follow leaders. *We know* that, you're saying. However, if you are not currently being considered a leader and you have no intention of becoming one, then you must rethink your wealth building strategy. There are of course some things you could do to become wealthy that do not require you to become a leader, however, once you are wealthy, then by default people will look to you for leadership. You might as well get used to it!

I realize that it may be difficult for you to accept the path of leadership for yourself, especially if it has not occurred to you. Have you ever considered the fact that business leaders do business with other business leaders, or that political leaders do business with other political leaders?

How do you create the perception of leadership if you have never been considered a leader before? Does someone come along and tap you on the shoulder and say, "Tag—you're a leader now"?

No.

You must create that perception yourself. Yes, you will get a lot of help along the way if you take on this responsibility, but you're the one who must begin the process.

One of the most effective ways to display leadership is to become an outstanding presenter. Where most are completely ineffective at presenting their ideas, strategies, techniques, and visions to other people, you must excel. Think about it: Most great leaders in history have been effective and passionate speakers. And if you really think about the people who you respect in business, are they not powerful presenters?

If you do not currently know how to effectively enrol and engage an audience, then it's time to learn.

The number one mistake that speakers make is to craft their presentations making it all about their information. Information, no matter how astounding, does not make a great presentation. You could have the greatest ideas and strategies on planet Earth, but if you are ineffective in presenting them and your audience is not affected by your presentation, your ideas will be lost.

Your content is your experience, knowledge, and expertise. But, I want to be very clear before going any further that your content is secondary to the context. Let me explain...

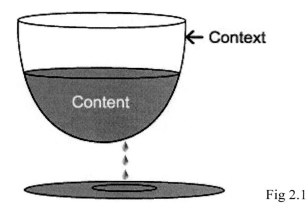

Fig 2.1

In Fig 2.1 you'll notice that inside the bowl is some water, and that water represents the content of your presentation. Your content is your experience and knowledge that you will share with your audiences. But even the tiniest of leaks will cause the whole of your content to leak out and be lost.

The bowl represents context— the framework you use to deliver your information. Most speakers and trainers try to share as much content as they can in the time they have. Whether it's for a 15-minute presentation or an entire day, most just spew out data, data, data! And, what has happened after five or ten minutes of boring data? Most of your audience has tuned out. They're either sleeping or daydreaming or checking their phones. They need context (represented by the bowl). The context is the way you transmit your information to those in attendance; it is literally the receptacle you use to pass the content over to them. If you have no context, you have no bowl. Have you ever tried to pass a litre of water to someone without using a receptacle of some sort? In other words, it's not what you have to say but whether what you're saying is getting across to your audience.

Did you know that most speakers are happy to have 20 percent of their audience paying attention? That's ridiculous. True leaders want 100 percent!

In order to achieve that, you need good context. One of the most powerful and fundamental tools you can use to create powerful context and deliver a highly enrolling and engaging presentation is Suggestology. You must become an expert Suggestologist. That means; learning to activate, amongst your audiences, their natural learning processes. If your audience feels part of the presentation, they'll engage with the content. If they're curious about what you're saying, they'll pay attention. If they're having fun, they'll listen. If they then learn something, they'll be motivated, engaged, and inspired!

We've talked quite a bit about Suggestology, and you have the broad strokes. But what is Suggestology exactly? It is a combination of asking questions and promoting learning through repetition. In my seminars I have learned several ways to do this. I can of course use it during the delivery of information, but I can also use it to respond to tough questions. In many cases, audience questions are meant to make the person asking the question look good. Not everybody likes being in an audience. When people feel as if their beliefs are being threatened or if they are insecure about the information the presenter is giving, the audience member will often lash out with tough questions meant to trip up the presenter.

Before I give you some powerful ways to use Suggestology, here is one way that I used it to handle an objection:

Not long ago, I had the opportunity to present a couple of hours of internet marketing strategies to just over 500 people in a large meeting room at a Toronto airport hotel. Things were going along nicely when, all of a sudden, someone in the audience to my left about halfway back put up their hand when I started talking about conversion pages. Conversion pages are webpages that sell. Now, I don't normally take questions in such a short presentation, but this particular person was insisting by holding up their hand for quite a long period of time. Finally, I sent the mic runner over to them, asked the audience member to stand up, at which point good context tells me to move to the opposite side of the stage towards the back in order to allow the audience member the floor. Making the audience the star is one way that I have learned to make them part of the presentation.

"Please stand and introduce yourself and state your question," I said.

He stood up immediately, brimming with confidence.

"Hi, my name is Roy, and I don't want you to take this the wrong way but..."

Uh oh, I thought. When somebody starts a question off with that, I know what their true purpose is—to find a way to make themselves look good by insulting my efforts. So, I braced myself with a smile for what was to come.

"...I did see your website. I've got to say—it's gaudy!"

Wow, I was floored. How could anybody have the audacity to stand up in front of 500 people and criticize the way my website looks. I knew that I was going to have to use every skill in my public speaking arsenal to keep from looking threatened and to keep the flow of the presentation heading in a positive direction.

What would you do in this situation? What would be your response?

That's where Suggestology comes in. You don't have to answer any questions or respond to threats. All you have to do is ask a question in response. That's what a good Suggestologist would do! They would think up the perfect question on the spot to disarm the attacker and get them to back off. What is the perfect question in this situation?

Would you ask, "Why do you say that it's gaudy?"

Would you ask, "What would you do to make it better?"

Would you ask, "What does gaudy mean, anyway?"

None of these are powerful response questions. Each of them allows the person with the microphone to convey a litany of reasons for their dislike of your website. I know my website is powerful because it gets results. That's the only thing that matters to me. Whether they dislike the web design or not is not really the issue.

So, I asked a question that did not allow them any room to manoeuvre. I asked, "Why did you go to my website in the first place?"

"I went there to find out if I should come to this seminar."

The audience broke into polite laughter. Obviously, my website did its job and pulled this person into my presentation. And just about the same time that they realized it, the guy with the microphone realized it, too.

"Does that answer your question?" I asked.

"Yes," was his answer.

"Okay! Thank you," I said. "Everyone give him a big hand." And they did.

Do you see how potentially bad that situation could have been? He could have thrown off my whole presentation, costing me thousands of dollars in potential future customers. Instead, I was able to flip his misplaced critique of my website into a selling point that brought the presentation to a new level of positivity, and I did it with Suggestology.

Asking a question hooks the mind and keeps it engaged. The mind has been programmed over and over again to immediately respond to questions, either mentally or verbally. In other words, if someone does not response to a question out loud does that mean their mind is not working on a response? No. The mind has been preconditioned to always respond to questions.

If your audience is engaged, then they will think more and learn more. When your audience tunes out due to a constant stream of data, they cannot learn at all. How can you be perceived as a leader if you are not helping your audience to learn or be inspired? For many years I did not know this. In my music career I would introduce pieces of music and tell the odd joke, but I never really felt like I was connecting with people. Questions are the ultimate connection tool. Why? Because an engaged mind is a connected mind. When you ask a steady series of questions, you are hooking the minds of your audience participants and the entire time they are buying into your presentation skills, which in turn create the perception of leadership.

What is the rule on using Suggestology in your presentations? Never go more than one minute without asking a question or soliciting some type of participation. People can't take more than one minute of constant information at a time. You must open something before you place something else into it; with that line of thought, you must open your audience's mind before you can teach them anything, and that is what Suggestology does!

Lesson—Becoming A Suggestologist

Here are four very powerful ways to use Suggestology in your presentations:

1. Anything you can state can be framed in the form of a question.

Consider the following statements.

Suggestology is the art of activating your natural will to learn.

How can you frame that statement in the form of an open-ended question designed to get others to think? Like this...

What is Suggestology?

Here is another example.

In order for you to create the perception of leadership, you must learn to become a powerful speaker.

How would you change this into an open-ended question? Here is one way.

How can you create the perception of leadership?

With practice you can get very good at asking open-ended questions. However, it *will* take practice.

2. Get others to finish your sentences.

This is equally as powerful as open-ended questions when it comes to soliciting audience response. Leaving the last word or phrase off the end of your sentences and gesturing to the audience for them to fill in the blanks is a powerful way to engage their minds. This is an even harder skill than asking open-ended questions, and is extremely rare to see in practice. I personally use it all the time and, while it may be difficult to implement in the beginning, once you get good at it you will see powerful results.

Here are some examples:

Leaving the last word or phrase off the end of your sentences is a great idea because it allows your audience to _____.

When giving powerful presentations try to remember that context is far more powerful than _____.

But what if they get the answer wrong? Guess what—it's not about them getting the answer right or wrong. If they answer the question, it means they are engaged. Any difference in responses will allow you to get ideas from different viewpoints. Their responses may even open up your presentation to a new discussion based on those different points of view.

3. Repeat the phrase and put "What?" at the end of the sentence.

This is an extremely effective and fun use of Suggestology. It gets your audience members to repeat important keywords or keyword phrases, further embedding the information into their subconscious and allowing them to learn faster and retain more.

Here are some examples:

Get your audience to fill in the blanks. Get your audience to fill in the what? "The blanks."

Never go longer than one minute without asking a question. Without asking a what? "A question."

4. Repeat the keyword or keyword phrase.

Much like number three, this use of Suggestology will get your audience to repeat important information, which is a practice that again allows that information to become embedded in their subconscious.

Here are some examples:

You should gesture to your audience when you want them to respond. What should you do? "Gesture to your audience."

It is extremely rare to see Suggestology in practice because it takes a lot of training and a lot of practice to get good at it. What does it take to get good at it? "A lot of training and practice."

As an aside, one of the most important things that you will have to remember that I have not discussed before is the use of the phrase, "Thank you." There's nothing like acknowledgment to keep your audience participating.

Every time you use Suggestology and you hear a response, or solicit a response from your audience you must say "thank you."

You say, "There are four very powerful ways of using suggestology."

Followed by, "how many ways?"

The audience responds, "Four."

To which you reply immediately by saying, "Thank you."

You've likely never done it before, because it is not a natural thing for any presenter to thank their audience during the presentation. You may see it at the end sometimes, but even then it is rare.

I have been doing this in my presentations for more than four years, and I can tell you that these two little words are perhaps the most powerful words in gaining trust, credibility, and respect from your audiences. It shows gratitude, humility, and respect.

Yes, I realize that this is unnatural and it may sound a lot easier than it actually is. But like anything that's worth doing, it's worth practicing. I encourage you to at least try it in your next presentation. Once it starts to flow and becomes natural, everyone will be affected by your presentation style and they'll love it. The result? The perceptions that others have of you will lean heavily towards you being a leader. When they're having fun and are engaged, they will automatically be drawn to your leadership.

Exercise—Suggestology Practice

Learning to insert Suggestology into your presentations will take practice and constant monitoring on your part to make sure that you are truly engaging your audiences.

In order to practice Suggestology it's a really good idea to start with your very next real life presentation. Start by writing down five key sentences that you would put into your next presentation. Even if you don't usually use notes, take the time to write down five key sentences that would most likely show up in your presentation.

Once you have those sentences, rewrite them using Suggestology. Please refer to the examples in this chapter. You have at your disposal four different ways of using Suggestology to transform your statements. What are they, again?

Anything you can state can be framed in the form of a question.

Get others to finish your sentences.

Repeat the phrase and put "What?" at the end of the sentence.

Repeat the keyword or keyword phrase.

Once you have your Suggestology-based sentences written out, practice them a few times before going live. Then, print them out in large print and take it with you to your next presentation. Place it somewhere near you so that you can refer to it when necessary.

Remember, leadership status is earned. The best way to earn that status is to build trust, credibility, and respect by using Suggestology in your presentations. Good luck with it—I know you'll do great.

Chapter 24—The Number One Rule of Successful Businesses

In almost every training session that I run, I ask one very important question: "What is the number one thing that you need to do in business to be successful?"

This question usually gets several responses such as perseverance, passion, commitment, a great team, big goals, ask for what you want, the ability to work long hours, thick skin, motivation, and so on. While these are all great answers, it's not the answer that I'm looking for. It's much simpler than that.

In order to be successful in business, what is the number one thing that you need to do?

SELL.

If you can't sell your products and services, then it's not a business—it's a hobby. Businesses rely on sales and cash flow. Yes, perhaps in the early days of an IPO or a big venture capital deal, you don't need to sell very much because you are in the start-up phase and you've got great ideas. But, even with great ideas, eventually you will need to create cash flow. And that means learning how to sell.

If you don't like selling, it's likely because you don't like being sold *to*. You are therefore projecting onto others how they should perceive your sales pitch. Because you want to people to think well of you, you resist selling something because you feel like you're invading somebody else's mental space.

If this is the way you feel, then consider this statement: You can't be good at something you don't like. If you absolutely hate sales, then my recommendation is you stay away from business. However, if you are open, then I would suggest to you that the reason you don't like selling is because you haven't really learned how.

Just like there is context in public speaking and presenting, there is also context in selling. It's not what you sell that matters, but "how" you sell that makes the difference. Many people believe that you either have it—good sales acumen, that is—or you don't. I prefer to believe that, like any other skill, you can learn to get good at sales. All you have to do is keep an open mind and learn from someone who knows how to sell.

Obviously, you should not take advice from well-meaning family and friends when it comes to sales if they cannot walk the walk. Only seek out those who are the best at it and have a system. Seek out those who have what you want.

For most of my adult life, I was not good at sales. Not at all. In fact, it would have been kind to call me horrible at it! I was never taught how to properly sell anything. I never knew that there were actually systems designed to help me sell and consequently the lack of a system created a lack in my sales. Now, after learning and practicing, I can say with complete honesty that I am good at what I do.

Most of what I do in the seminar business and in the training business is selling. Yes, it is important to have good information, up-to-date concepts and skills and a great delivery system. Still, I know lots of people who have that and don't do very well financially because they simply don't know how to sell what they've got. Does that sound like anybody you know? What I found very interesting is that most of those who don't do well financially don't want to learn how to sell, either. They would prefer to take a backseat and let somebody else do the selling. Now consider the fact that leaders are selling their viewpoints and their systems. If you truly want to be considered a leader because you know that is your quickest route to financial success then you, too, must learn to sell.

Several chapters ago I talked about an experience that I had selling 422 CDs at a single concert. That was not an accident. It was a system at work. Once I started implementing that same system in everything that I did, the results were truly miraculous.

One of the first things that I offered to businesses, when I started up my training company, was to help others learn Internet marketing. Learning internet marketing is one of the most important things to learn in today's world. It is no longer 1999; it is the early 2000s, and if you don't know how to market your product on the information superhighway, you are going to have a hard time competing in a global market. I still find it amazing how much confusion there is in the marketplace as to how Internet marketing actually works. There are fundamental concepts, which are still relatively unknown by many people. In the beginning I felt that a good one-day hands-on training course was enough to get the information across. But what I quickly learned is that people can only absorb so much information at one time. So I switched to a two-day intensive training course. The cost for this course was $997.

I will never forget one of the early two-day weekend Internet marketing seminars that I conducted. It was for approximately 20 people. It seems to me that most of the business people in that course were having a good time and learning a great deal. But there was one gentleman, who looked to be in his 50s, who sat in the front row to my right for the entire two days and didn't ask a single question. He also looked disinterested for the most part. He was attentive and taking a lot of notes, but he just didn't seem that outgoing. You know how you look at people sometimes and you think to yourself *It just doesn't look like they're that happy.* That's what I felt about this particular gentleman. I really didn't know if he was learning anything or if he felt like it was a complete waste of time. I knew that he was a professional marketer with a big company, but I didn't know much more than that about him. You have to consider the fact that I was still relatively new to training and, even though I had a great deal of Internet marketing experience, I didn't really know how businesses would respond. Had they heard it all before?

Late in the second day of the training, I opened up the floor to questions or anything that the participants wanted to discuss. It was then that this gentleman raised his hand and I asked him to stand up.

He started off by saying, "you know Paul... I have been to literally dozens of seminars in my career."

Uh oh, I thought. Here we go.

He continued, "While some of the seminars and training that I've attended have been good and some have been not-so-good, I just had one thing to give you some feedback about this one. One thing I think you've done completely wrong on your end."

I braced for what came next.

"I really think that you should raise your prices," he exclaimed.

"Really?" I responded with a more than surprised look on my face. "What do you think I should charge?"

"Well, based on what other people are charging in the marketplace, you should at least double your prices because I have received at least double the amount of value of any training I have ever participated in and I've paid sometimes ten times as much as you're charging. So, if that gives you any indication of what you should be charging, then I hope that helps you." He finished.

"Thank you," I said. "Everyone give him a big hand." And I truly meant that.

I was actually pretty happy and impressed with myself that I was getting $1000 per person for two days of training.

Was it possible that I could shift my mind to believe that my work was even more valuable?

About a week later, Nancy and I were driving to a preview presentation in Hamilton, Ontario. During the drive, which was approximately half an hour, we discussed the prices of our seminars the entire time. We were of course concerned that if we charged too much money, people would respond negatively. The conversation went back and forth for several minutes, between keeping our rates the same and moving them up in price. There were arguments in favour of both sides. It is safer to keep the rates the same and get the same conversion percentages that we were used to. But the thought of actually doubling our rates seemed like a challenge. It was then that we thought, "What's the worst that can happen?" People don't buy in. Then all we have to do next time is put the rates back to what we're used to until we feel more confident. It was then that we decided to double the rates for this seminar in Hamilton and let the chips fall where they may.

During my presentation in Hamilton, I was projecting myself towards the close. It was uncharted territory. However, I just detached from the experience: If it worked, it worked; if it didn't, I learned something. Before I knew it, the final 15 minutes of the seminar were upon me. I transitioned from the information portion of my seminar to offering a new 3-day advanced Internet marketing course. I figured if I charged a bit more I could add some more information and for that, I'd need another day. When it came time to write the actual tuition on the flipchart, I turned my back to the audience, grabbed a marker and paused.

The time was upon me to make a decision. Everything before this, all the talking, all the pros and cons lists—they had all been practice. Do I remain status quo or do I take a chance? It was then that I did something that I'll never forget. I didn't double the price of my seminar. I couldn't. My hands wouldn't let me.

I tripled it.

After writing the number on the flipchart, I turned around and looked at the audience. They didn't look any different than before. Nobody gasped in horror and nobody got up and ran for the door.

Maybe this will work, I thought. Maybe I have been selling myself short all this time.

That day, I sold the same conversion percentage as before yet, this time, I was getting three times the amount of money per person. Wow! It's true what I had been taught. It's not what you sell but *how* you sell it that really matters.

Sometimes when you raise your prices, people actually see your product as more valuable. And guess what? It *is* true. You are the arbiter of prices when it comes to the unique knowledge you have to share, and if you can charge double or triple what you're charging now, and people are willing to pay that much for it, does it not mean that your product is more valuable than it was before? Think about what you charge your clients and consider raising your prices. What's the worst that could happen? I can tell you that you may lose the clients who are bleeding you dry and not paying you very much in favour of clients who are far easier to work with because they truly see the value in what you do.

I gave this information to one of my coaching students, who was trying to start up an internet marketing business. While the business got rolling, he still did full-time work carving headstones for funeral homes. He didn't mind the work, but he'd rather do something else and that's why he's my coaching student. His goal was to get his internet business to replace his full-time income so that he could work far less and get paid at least the same amount.

My recommendation was not to wait for the internet marketing business to pick up. He could actually create more time now by charging more money to his headstone clients. I asked him, "How many competitors do you have that are good at doing what you do?"

He replied, "Not that many."

"Then what would be the harm in raising your prices? What else are your clients going to do? If you really are that good at what you do, then they should be willing to pay more—would you agree with that?"

He agreed and asked, "How much do you think I should raise the prices?"

"Well, based on what you've told me, at least 20 percent." I proclaimed confidently.

"Oh my, that seems like a lot," He said hesitantly.

"Try to remember that you are valued in what you do. I don't think you will encounter any problem. They'll just pay the extra 20 percent."

While he was not sure that he could do it, he promised me that he would think about it. Then, when he was in my office yesterday for his coaching session, he told me that he increased his fees by 15 percent. He simply didn't feel that 20 percent would be acceptable, and he wasn't comfortable charging that much money.

"What happened?" I asked.

"Nobody said a word," he said with a big smile on his face.

"Told you."

He also told me that he let go of a couple of low-paying clients because he just didn't have the time to deal with them anymore and, because of the new rate change, he didn't really need them anyway. So he got the best of **both** worlds: He now works less and gets paid more. Talk about becoming a deliberate creator!

If you are worried about losing clients if you up your rates, then consider this: When you lose a client, it creates a void in the universe that needs to be filled. And usually what happens is that it will be filled with a better client. Let the people who are draining you go, and deal with the ones who you want to do business with—the ones who see your value.

Lesson—How To Sell vs Getting Others to Buy

The biggest lesson you could learn about selling is that you shouldn't be selling. Instead, you should be using a system to get others to buy. This is a complete shift in mindset.

There is always a game of skeptical volleyball playing itself out in the head of a potential customer. It's a game between cost and value. In order for you to succeed, value needs to beat cost. I recommend that you be the best at what you do so that you can charge the most. Then, all you have to do is use the system that I'm about to give you to get them to see *only* the value.

How can you get them to see only the value? Well, the only thing on planet Earth that is bigger than their skepticism is whether they feel something for you or your products. You *have* to get them to feel something. If you can't get them to feel strongly about your products and services based on the benefits that they will be receiving, then it will be very difficult to charge the money you want to charge. This is actually very empowering information. If you truly think about it, that's all you have to do: get them to feel good. The first thing you need to do is build some trust. You do business with people you trust, don't you?

The Ultimate Sales Template

The following sales template will not only help you build trust, but the context is so powerful that when you adopt it, practice it, and implement it, you could easily see your sales soar immediately. I can count on this particular sales template to convert a minimum of 30 percent. I've even done 100 percent on occasion depending on the situation. What would a 30 percent conversion rate mean to your business? That means that, for every hundred people who come across your path, 30 of them buy. That's huge.

Even though the first part of your sales presentation is important, the purpose of this sales template is to walk you through the close. Throughout the first part of your presentations, you earn the trust of your prospect, deliver some value, build some credibility, and get them to like you. People do business with people they know, respect, trust, and like.

When you feel it's time to make the close, follow this template.

Problem/Solution

Come up with what you believe to be their biggest problem and then offer up the solution—your product or service. Sometimes your prospects don't know or cannot put their finger on their own problems. What you need to do is devise a really good one or two sentence explanation of what you believe to be their problem.

Let's say you're talking to a small business and your solution to their web dilemma is search engine optimization services. You could say the following:

"In my experience, the biggest problem facing most small businesses like yours is not nearly enough qualified and targeted traffic from important sources like Google."

Then you would offer up the solution—your search engine optimization services:

"The solution for you would be choosing five highly searched and highly targeted keyword phrases that represent your products and services. Then, all you would need is to implement a systematic yet one hundred percent organic back link strategy over the next six months."

Then it's very important that you ask the following:

"Is it okay if I tell you about it?"

Consider the power of this question. What does it do?

Asking permission breaks down their defenses and puts them at ease. If they say yes, (which, by the way, they always do), then they have subconsciously given you permission to sell to them. Psychologically, this is huge. Getting their permission to sell to them is like a wolf getting the keys to a henhouse. It's brilliant!

Once you get their permission, remember to say, "Thank you."

Now get your game face on and follow this approach:

Who is it for?

Tell your prospect who normally qualifies for your products or services. This is also subliminal and is known as the "qualify close". Describe several types of individuals or businesses who utilize your services and products. This list will include your prospect.

If you are talking about SEO services you could say the following:

"The types of businesses and people who utilize our services and have had success are small to medium-sized business owners, marketing managers, sales professionals, and professional marketers."

Be sure to mention their position among the list of qualified people. When they hear their position and/or title, then they will subconsciously feel they qualify, as well, and be primed to accepting your product as something they'd like to purchase.

What's In It For Them

Present to them a list of what your product does and its key benefits. This is a good opportunity to get very clear on the values and benefits of your products and services. Write these valuable aspects of your product out and have them on-hand in list form.

Let's go back to our search engine optimization seminar. To your prospect you could say the following:

"You will learn the following: how to do targeted keyword research in a minimum amount of time so that you can come up with the most highly searched and least competitive keyword phrases for your website; how to place these keyword phrases effectively on each of your webpages so that Google recognizes their value and ranks them higher in its search engine results pages; and how to build anchor text back links to your website so that the Google search engine algorithm can see your website has ranked well in terms of 'off-site' optimization."

You can make the list fairly long if there are a lot of deliverables. Just be sure to make each bullet point include these parts: what your product does, what it will do, what they will learn, and its key benefits.

Testimonials

Always carry with you a stack of written testimonials from satisfied customers. Simply read three or four of them for your prospect. This will satisfy any doubts that they have about the quality of your service. If you do not have any testimonials, then *e-mail previous clients and satisfied customers and request some of them.*

And bring more than you plan to read. Often in my seminars, when I am up-selling another course, I will read three or four testimonials and then people will come up after the seminars and read through the stack that I have left on the front table. Essentially what they're looking for is more evidence to make up their minds. Which way do you think they will sway to if the evidence they find is a glowing review from someone they know or a leading industry expert?

Introduce Future Bonuses

This is your opportunity to introduce products and/or services that are less of an investment for your prospect. Initially, it will give them the opportunity to do business with you for less investment. However, what you intend to do is to include these products and/or services—at the right time—in the entire package.

Come up with products and/or services complementary to your main product. If you are selling an advanced Internet marketing training course, then you could talk about complementary pre-recorded training products. You could say something like this:

"One possible solution for people that want to learn at their own pace and do not have the time to attend our courses is to study online through our advanced online training videos. There is one specific product entitled 'Twelve Essential Lessons on Internet Marketing.' In this course you will learn step-by-step information on how to build your own website, maximize the content, do targeted keyword research, build a mailing list, and more! The cost of this product is $497."

Don't feel too compelled to figure out bonuses to your actual program. However, consider the fact that people become more motivated to purchase when you pile on the value. Sometimes in my courses, people struggle to come up with bonuses. I'm not going to go through the list of everything that they have come up with, but, when they work together with teams, they always come up with *something*. And, you can, too. You just have to put some thought into it!

This type of sale strategy plays into the "buy one, get one free" mentality - the biggest pulling offer in history. People are definitely motivated by extra value.

Deal

Depending on the situation and circumstance of the sale, feel free to discount your service and/or product. People buy when things are on sale. Yes, I hear what you're saying: "My price is my price."

I get that. I do. You do not have to discount your products drastically, but giving them a little deal will grease the wheels and get things rolling. People will see it as a kind gesture on your part and an opportunity to participate.

Bonuses

This is where you would include, in the sale of your big product and/or service, the future bonuses that you introduced before. You could say something like this: "Right now, when you purchase [PRODUCT A], I will include all of the other products that I mentioned, as well, which have a value of $997." It is important to put a solid dollar figure on the bonuses so that people see them as valuable.

Limitation

There are really only two types of limitations: time and quantity. Put the time limitation on your bonus at a day, or a week. Whatever you decide, just make sure you have some sort of time limit or people will do what most people do when they have time to think—procrastinate. If they go home and feel they have all the time in the world to decide whether to get your product, the initial energy you instilled in them and your whole presentation's focus goes down the drain. Your closing ratio will drop dramatically once people leave. Do your best to close the deal on the spot.

Also, let your prospects know that sometimes the demand outweighs the supply. If business is going great, simply let your prospects know that if they don't act immediately they could miss out or be put on a waiting list.

Guarantee

There are two types of guarantees: conditional and unconditional. Obviously an unconditional guarantee means that you will refund 100 percent of their money should any problem arise whatsoever. The conditional guarantee means you will refund a portion of their money or that certain conditions have to be carried out in order for them to request a refund. In either case, your sales will increase dramatically if you have a guarantee. Based upon the small percentage of refunds that you will give, the amount of sales that you will make will far outweigh the refunds, which are simply the cost of doing more business. Incidentally, the technical term that describes the effectiveness of the guarantee is called *risk reversal*. Essentially you are taking the risk off of the buyer and putting it onto yourself.

Close

Explain your payment options and how you will accept payment. If you have payment plans then lay them out quickly. Otherwise, tell them what types of payment you will accept and put a piece of paper in front of them to sign. In most cases they will have questions, however, because you waited until the last possible minute to make the sale, impress upon them that your time is limited and, while you will take a few questions, you do not have time to go over the whole presentation again. You might get a question that you can't answer on the spot or that might visibly shake you, and this will put him doubt in the prospect's heads. Let them know that you have to leave soon and that you highly recommend that they take the deal.

Exercise—Putting It to the Test

I have used this closing template a few thousand times. Each time I do it I am amazed at its power. Typically, a 30 percent close is the minimum for products under $1,000. That number is reduced to between 20 and 30 percent for products in the $3,000 range. That's an amazing conversion percentage.

Think about how this would revolutionize your business and create more cash flow. Do you think you could use that sort of bump in your sales? I highly encourage you to test this out as soon as possible. Think about when your next sales presentation is and follow this powerful closing template exactly. Then, watch the magic happen.

Chapter 25—Marketing Comes First

A few years ago I had the opportunity to attend the National Publicity Summit in New York. This is a media conference put on by Steve Harrison that attracts high-level media outlets and industry leaders who are seeking media attention. Some of the media outlets in attendance were large organizations such as FOX news, CNBC, *Rachel Ray*, *The View*, *Good Morning America*, the *Wall Street Journal*, *New York Times*, and various other TV, radio, print, and online media companies.

I didn't necessarily have anything to promote at the time, but the conference was a learning opportunity on how to package my products and services and promote them to media channels. Most if not all of the attendees had books to promote. In fact, many of the attendees had several books, and I seemed to be the only one in the room among the hundred delegates looking for media attention who didn't. This turned out to be a blessing, because many of the things that I learned about what the media actually wants have made it into *this* book.

Sure, I was a bit envious of the other participants who had books, but for some reason I became the one giving out loads of advice to the other participants. If I didn't have a book, then why was I so busy? Well, most of the participants, even though they had books, weren't making much money from their books! Getting publicity is one thing, but making money from it is another thing entirely. I learned that a book was a high-priced business card and, unless you're extremely lucky, incredibly talented, or can manifest deliberately several million book sales, then you'll need to learn the method of making money as an expert in your field. The perception amongst the other delegates was that I was successful as a marketer, and they all wanted to pick my brain on how to do it for themselves. How could I say no? I gladly helped those who asked for it.

For the most part, their questions surrounded the concept of online marketing—things like how to build a profitable website, generate leads, convert consulting clients, and attract corporate training contracts were among the top questions. I quickly realized that my experience with marketing was valuable, and many of the things that I talked about with them made it into this book. To be a successful marketer you will have to be outstanding in a diverse number of areas. But, as I always state, there are certain things far more important than others. In the beginning, the most important pieces of the puzzle are to create the perception of expertise in your field and dominate your market place. I will talk about these things specifically in the lesson portion of this chapter. For now, we will focus on the conference itself and my experiences at the National Publicity Summit. It's important to realize that there is more to capturing the attention of the media than whether you have a book that you've written under your arm or not.

The conference basically worked like this: days one and two involved training sessions on how to present yourself to the media, and days three and four were set aside to actually present to them in a speed-dating kind of format. My initial goal was of course to learn what the media look for in terms of stories that would capture their attention. I really didn't feel prepared to meet the media. I knew that they were looking for great stories, but more often than not what they require is a book to qualify your expertise. Yet, regardless of the fact that I didn't have that book I did get a couple of high-level meetings, which I was not expecting. The first was with CNBC and the second was with *The View*. If you're not familiar with these media outlets, CNBC is a powerful television and online business news and business affairs channel. *The View* is a popular talk show hosted by top media personalities Barbara Walters, Whoopi Goldberg, Joy Behar, Elisabeth Hasselbeck, and Sherri Shepherd.

CNBC was looking for experts in the areas of online marketing. Wow, what luck! I seemed to be one of the few people in the room who knew all about that.

Only a couple of people out of a hundred got the opportunity to speak with CNBC, and only three got a meeting with *The View*. What a privilege! What I learned at the media conference got me those meetings. Obviously, it's good to come to the table with a little bit of experience, but as I've mentioned before in this book, it's not what you present that matters—it's how you do it.

In both cases, in the 2 1/2 minutes that I had to present, I focused on what was in it for them and targeted my message directly towards their audiences. I was as surprised as anyone when I was summoned to the private meetings. In fact, quite innocently, I think I said to Jeffrey from CNBC, "Why me?"

Here's what *The View* producers told me. "We're not going to put you on The View."

I wondered why we were meeting, if that were the case.

Then they said "Yet."

That sounded interesting. What does "Yet" mean?

"We want you to let us know when you have a book, but even then we won't put you immediately on *The View*. If you mess up on national television, then your career is over. So we'll get you some interviews with local affiliates and, if you do well there, we'll consider you for *The View*, " they explained.

Wow, that's good advice, I thought. It's amazing when you take risks how much you actually learn about the way things work. They were actually looking out for me and letting me know how the system works—helping me learn the ins and outs of exactly what I needed to do to get the publicity I was after.

The reason why I'm letting you know this is because, like Steve Harrison says, "When you put yourself in the position to be famous, you can do pretty much anything you want." There is no question in my mind that publicity will help your situation as it is helping mine. But the real message is *don't write the book first.* The first thing you should do is walk your walk. Many people write books before they are ready. They write books based on research and case studies and, while some good books are made that way, you will have to know how to walk your walk before you convince anyone to buy it.

Many of the other delegates at that conference, even though they had books, were not getting the attention that they wanted. Perhaps the reason for that is that a book doesn't necessarily make you an expert—experience does!

As I mentioned, many of the delegates at the conference were picking my brain in terms of my online marketing strategies. They wanted to know how they could leverage their books to build successful business. A book, they realized, is not a business, nor is it a marketing tool unless you know how to turn it into one. The rules of online marketing are very specific. Knowing them and practicing them could make the difference between your success and your failure.

Lesson—The Big Online Marketing Picture

Whether you call it online marketing, digital marketing, Internet marketing, or even e-commerce, the aim is the same: to use the Internet to market your products and services effectively so that you can build leads, convert sales, and grow your business. Since entering into the online marketing world in a serious way in 2006, I have attended dozens of conferences, taken several training courses, and put in countless hours of work into my own online marketing projects. I've sold everything from sheet music to online piano lessons, taught everything from online business study courses to webinars, and hosted everything from training courses to consulting services. To be successful online requires what I call the "Four Pillars of Internet Marketing": targeted keyword research, traffic, engagement, and conversion.

Your goal is to go after an already existing targeted audience online, bring them to your website, communicate with them in a way that engages them, and convert their interest into business. Let's talk about each one of the strategies one at a time.

Targeted Keyword Research

While most businesses recognize that the internet is one of the most important marketing avenues for any product or service, what most of them don't realize is; actually how to go about *using it*. The biggest mistake most of them make is going out and blindly hiring a web designer, thinking that marketing is not their own responsibility. Nothing could be further from the truth. While certain web designers may have some marketing skills, they are hired to design your website, not market your product. Having said that, you must recognize that it is your responsibility to educate yourself on exactly what internet marketing is and how to go about it.

Keyword research is essentially the art of discovering highly targeted keyword phrases that represent your content. This means finding keyword phrases that get a lot of searches but have relatively little competition. Picking keyword phrases by guessing is *not* a good idea. Even though the keyword phrases that you and your colleagues come up with may seem logical, they still need to be tested to see if they meet the parameters of keyword phrases that will attract traffic from major search engines. Of course, the most important search engine is Google. There are literally trillions of websites out there, which means you better believe you'll have competition. Effective search engine optimization starts with targeted keyword research to determine whether or not your keyword phrases will be effective vehicles to show up in a Google search engine results page.

Determining effective keyword phrases means understanding how Google works. When someone types in a keyword phrase into Google's search box, what actually happens? How does Google determine who makes it to the top of the search results?

Google bases its organic search results on two main factors: *on-site optimization* and *off-site optimization*. On-site optimization considers how a keyword phrase is represented in your website's content. Off-site optimization looks at the determining factors outside of your website that help your site pages rank higher.

Let's start with on-site optimization. You must take a keyword phrase and place it in strategic positions within your website so that Google can recognize that your content is reflective and relevant to that keyword phrase. Essentially the most important areas to put your keyword phrase are in the title tag, description, URL and head or H1 tag. When Google finds the keyword phrase in these areas its elder rhythm says to itself, "This page is about this keyword phrase." And then your webpage enters into competition with all the other webpages out there that use the same or similar keyword phrases. One thing is for certain: If you do not have the keyword phrase anywhere on your website, it is very unlikely that you will show up in the search results for that keyword phrase.

Websites that take a sophisticated approach to search engine optimization understand the value of placing the keyword phrase in appropriate places. There have been many discussions about the amount of times your keyword phrase should appear in your content, and many search engine optimization experts believe that keyword density is not one of the determining factors of search engine placement. However, my belief is that your content should reflect the keyword phrase as much as possible while not seeming too spammy. In other words, don't put the keyword phrase into your content more than seems natural. Another good rule of thumb is to keep your keyword density below five percent. (All that means is that a phrase should not appear in your content more than five percent of the time based on the total number of words.)

Off-site optimization deals with how many other online properties endorse your website by putting what is known as a *back link* to your webpage on their own site. Many people think that you will rank higher in Google search results pages if you get more traffic. That is one of the biggest myths of the Internet. Google doesn't actually know how much traffic you get, and so it would be unfair and unrealistic to rank on that factor. It knows how much traffic it sends you, but does it really know how much traffic you get from Yahoo or Facebook? Not necessarily.

A back link is essentially a hyperlink from someone else's website to yours. And, for that back link to seem of value to Google, the website that gives you the back link must have a good amount of back links of its own. If you have a back link from a website that is relatively new, it will not be as powerful in promoting your ranking in search engines as having a back link from a website that has been around for a long time and has several thousand back links of its own.

Entire books have been written on search engine optimization alone. For now, it suffices to know that if on-site optimization and off-site optimization are the key factors in determining where your website shows up in Google search engine results pages, then those two aspects are big determiners of your success online. Wouldn't it be great to have software that could show you what your competition is up to as it pertains to these key factors? Of course. And that software is called Market Samurai.

Here's how it works:

You give Market Samurai a category, an idea, a phrase, a product name, or whatever it is that you want to rank for, and the software will access Google's AdWords database and deliver you a lengthy targeted list of other keyword phrases that you would have never thought to incorporate that will help your standings. Market Samurai gives you an extended list of keyword phrases that people type into Google, saving you literally hundreds of hours of work.

You then analyze those keyword phrases based on the number of searchers per day, the amount of competition that there is online for that keyword phrase, and a few other important areas such as Phrase-to-Broad Ratio, and SEOT, so that you can narrow the keyword phrases to the most effective ones for your website.

The third step in this process is to analyze a few targeted keyword phrases in depth based on who currently holds the top ten spots on Google.com. What are they do to rank so high? Most importantly, what are they *not* doing? Market Samurai will enlighten you to the on-site and off-site optimization strategies of your competition so that you can quickly determine the most suitable keyword phrase to use on your new webpage, blog post, or YouTube video.

Guessing keywords is not an option. You must do research and use the right tools in order to reach the top of a Google search engine results page, or at least be on the consumer's radar by placing on the first ten pages.

To watch a video on Market Samurai in action and to download a free 12-day trial of this amazing software, please visit the following URL:

http://www.trainingbusinesspros.com/m/seo-keyword-research

Traffic

Search engine optimization is your most important long-term traffic source. It may cost you some time in building effective webpages that reflect good keyword phrases and building back links to your site, but this can be done in as little as 20 minutes per day. Your most important search engine optimization traffic rule is to create relevant content on an ongoing basis and build back links to that new content.

What are some other important traffic sources? Here are some of the things that you could consider as effective traffic builders:

Pay Per Click Advertising: Popular search engines like Google, Yahoo, Bing and social media giants like Facebook and LinkedIn have programs where you can purchase paid search engine results listings based on the amount of money that you pay per click through to your website. This is a very powerful strategy to determine whether your webpage that you've created actually has the desired conversion effect. In other words, if you pay for traffic and send it directly to your webpage and you don't make money or build leads, then you know that the webpage needs to be changed to get the desired effect.

Social media networks: With the popularity of social media networks such as Facebook, LinkedIn, Twitter, YouTube, Docstoc, Scribd, Flicker, Reddit, Digg, Delicious, Myspace, Foursquare, Pinterest, etc. it has become more important than ever to learn social media strategies from a communications, branding, and traffic building perspective. I could literally write an entire book about building traffic using social media channels, but here are some quick rules to follow when creating content: refrain from hard selling, and makes sure to deliver value, build curiosity, engage in conversation, increase your connections, and get others talking about your company. Social media is not so much about you delivering your messages but getting other people to deliver it through recommendations of you or your product to their peer group. I highly recommend you attend one of our social media training sessions or purchase one of our online advanced social media home study courses, as cracking into social groups is anything but simple.

Press releases and article marketing: These are great way to get your content spread across multiple websites and increase brand awareness. Create some valuable content for popular sites like PRWeb or eZineArticles.com and you will notice an increase in traffic when people read your articles and click the links in your bio to get more information on the concepts and strategies that you write about.

Off-line marketing: Traditional marketing methods such as TV, radio, print, or even grassroots marketing concepts like flyers and networking meetings are a great way to build traffic to your site. Always include your website address with your marketing material with a call to action and a reason for people to visit your site.

Enrol and Engage

When someone hits your website, how long do you think you actually have to capture their attention to enrol and engage them? About 15 seconds. It still amazes me how few websites are actually good at this! Having trained thousands of businesses I see it all too often: The biggest thing on company XYZ's website is their logo and their company name. That may be okay if you are a big brand company, but if no one knows your brand then why would you put yourself first? They should come first. The first thing you're your website should do is explain in under 15 seconds of reading time what's in it for them (WIIFM).

The most powerful way to capture a reader's interest is to put a powerful hypnotic headline in the prime real estate section of your webpage. Which area is prime real estate? The top center of the page is considered prime real estate because it is the place that captures the attention of the eye. I first came across the concept of hypnotic headlines and hypnotic copywriting from a well-known marketer named Joe Vitale. According to Joe and to the results that I'm getting with my own online marketing projects, a great hypnotic headline is the perfect way to capture someone's interest. What is hypnotic copywriting? It is writing that captures attention, engages the reader, and converts interest into sales. In short, it is "copywriting that sells" or "salesmanship in print". If you write in a manner that uses key contextual elements, you will hook the reader into a focused mental state where the only thing that matters is *what comes next.*

One of the myths of good copywriting is that it is somehow *spontaneous combustion.* Nothing could be further from the truth. Good hypnotic copywriting requires adhering to specific rules and techniques. Even experienced copywriters take a fair bit of time they need to create good copy for a website. It takes experience to learn what a reader responds to, what their fears, are and connect with them. If you cannot connect with your reader then they will be distracted by something more interesting than your website. If the reader gets bored they will abandon your site, and the sale is lost.

Hypnotic copywriting is essentially Suggestology in print. In order to activate the natural will of your reader to keep reading and learn something, you will have to connect with the way they make decisions. People make decisions subconsciously based on how they feel. If your copywriting does not make them feel anything, then you will be unsuccessful at hooking their attention and capturing their interest. Your copywriting needs to be persuasive enough to get the reader to take action. The ultimate key to becoming a great hypnotic copywriter is to always practice your copywriting skills. I have made the mistake of creating webpages that have little to no effect on the reader. All I need to do is go back and change the format and writing to adhere to the tenets of hypnotic copywriting, and more often than not this lifts client accumulation dramatically.

Here are the top 10 things to keep in mind when creating hypnotic headlines for your webpages:

Grab the reader's attention immediately by making your headline big, bold, and in the top center of your webpage.

The eye will naturally be drawn to this prime real estate section of your webpage.

Inform them that they're in the right place. You can do this by including the same keyword phrase on the main page that you used to bring your readers from search engines. For example, if you optimize your webpage for the keyword phrase "advanced piano lessons", then you must use that same keyword phrase in your headline. This tells the reader that they've landed in the right place and compels them to continue exploring your site.

The most important element of hypnotic copywriting is to create curiosity. Curiosity is the basis for all subconscious attention. When the mind is curious the power of suggestion and persuasion is activated. The power of Suggestology kicks in, activates the subconscious, and draws their attention. What is one of the best ways to hook the curiosity of the reader? By asking a question or a series of questions meant to hook the mind and keep it engaged.

Get your reader to feel something. Ask yourself, "What is it we're really selling?" Are we selling piano lessons or are we selling the feeling of playing great piano? Are we selling a car or are we selling the feeling of driving in luxury on an open highway? Are we selling recipes or are we selling the ability to make great food? Once you know what it is you're really selling, you can create the hypnotic copywriting to support it. Think of the benefit instead of the product. Think of the results before the how-to.

When I ask you to think of the word "whale", what comes to mind? Shamu? Killer? Beluga? Open ocean? Fin? Underwater? What does this simple exercise prove?

People think in pictures. In your copywriting use words that get your reader to picture something in their mind. And, just to prove that the power of imagery and pictorial suggestion is powerful, I didn't really ask you to think of a whale, I asked you to think of the word w-h-a-l-e. And likely you skipped right over the word "word" and went straight to picturing a whale in your mind.

Two of the most powerful words in copywriting are the words "Yeah, sure!" People are inherently skeptical especially if you overstate what seems likely. Yes, it is important in your headlines to make your product or service seem special, but do not overdo it! If people are generally skeptical and if after reading your headline they say to themselves, "Yeah, sure", then they will likely abandon the webpage. Have you ever been to one of those webpages that exclaims, "This is not a scam"? What is the first thing that pops into your head? "Yeah, sure!" One of the best ways to avoid this thought by your reader is to never make your claim bigger than your proof.

Imagine for a moment that you are climbing Mount Everest when you look down and realize that, instead of remembering to put on your hiking boots, you're wearing sandals. Now think website copy. Trying to capture someone's interest on a webpage without hypnotic copywriting is trying to scale Mount Everest in flip-flops. What is this hypnotic strategy? Metaphor. Metaphor is a way of capturing interest by piecing together two seemingly unrelated objects. Use popular sources like fictional stories, sports, fairy tales, or even movies as your metaphor fuel.

Round up your audience. One of the best ways to capture the interest of your target market and get them to pay attention is to "call them by name". If someone sees their profession, title, or demographic in print, it immediately captures their attention and coaxes their interest because they think to themselves, *Hey, this webpage is talking about me.*

Use the "5W1H" formula. This is a formula often used by journalists when investigating and compiling their stories. It means who, what, why, when, where and how.

Who are you advertising to?

What does your product do for them?

Why is it superior to other similar products?

Where should you advertise to reach your target audience?

When is the best time to reach them?

How can you prove your case?

If you can answer these questions with your copywriting, then you will be successful in hooking interest, building curiosity, and closing the deal.

Say or promote the unexpected. When headlines start out one way then shift in another direction abruptly causing the reader to shift their focus in a humorous or sometimes surprising way, then you have succeeded in standing out. For example, the following is a headline I created for myself which I often use in my seminars as an example of achieving the unexpected and hooking interest.

"Jazz Musician Avoids Bankruptcy by Becoming a Millionaire."

Conversion

This is by far and away the most difficult part of internet marketing. Capturing leads and converting sales are the lifeblood of any company because sales create cash flow and in business cash flow is king. If you get really good at hypnotic copywriting, you can convert a website visitor into a sale the very first time. However, that will take a lot of practice and a significant amount of time formulating powerful sales pages. Yet, it is still not the most powerful conversion strategy. What is? The money's in the list!

The goal of list marketing is to capture a lead and convert that lead over time. The goal is to build trust, credibility, and respect by delivering a series of high value topics to your readers through the use of automation. The e-mail marketing version of automation is called an auto responder. There are several online services which are pay-per-subscriber services, and there is software you can install through your website service provider that will automate the process.

Essentially the strategy is this: get people to opt into your subscription list and then they will receive a high value series of e-mail responses. In my experience you should not deliver everything that they've opted into immediately. Do it over time. You could send an e-mail a day for the first six days, and then switch it to once a week. The obvious reason for building a mailing list is that people don't buy when you're ready to sell. Building an auto response campaign is a very inexpensive way to capture leads and convert those leads over time. People will obviously need a reason to join your mailing list. I can't tell you how many times I've been to somebody's website and I see a little box that reads "Join our mailing list." How pathetic! People do not give up their e-mail addresses these days for nothing. You have to explain what's in it for them in the headline of your opt-in subscription box.

Here are some examples of headlines from my opt-in subscription boxes on my websites:

The Top Six Public Speaking Mistakes And How To Avoid Them

The Top Six Most Popular Sheet Music Pieces Free

How To Make Google Your Sales Force

Tobeyisms—What's New And What's Not In Marketing

Once people opt in to your subscription list and they receive some good value from you, they will learn to trust you. Then, when you have a new program, a product that you want to promote, or an event that you want them to attend, simply send them a new hypnotic e-mail to promote it. They will be more open to receiving it if they have received good value from you in the past.

Essentially what you're doing is building a targeted subscription list of people who are interested in your products and services and once in a while using that list to promote something for sale. The key to making the sale is not to use your e-mails to sell but rather to include a link in your e-mail that leads back to your website. If you really want to increase your conversions, don't sell to your list too often. Wait until you have something highly valuable to promote and then send an e-mail that describes the value of the product or service and what's in it for them. But don't talk sales. Instead, put a link at the end of the e-mail that reads, "Click here to learn more." That link should lead them back to the webpage where you can sell as hard as you want using hypnotic copywriting.

Why is this the most effective conversion technique? Because people do business with people they trust. Use your mailing list to build that trust over time, and you will be extremely happy with the amount of sales that trust can bring you.

Exercise—Create Your Award-Winning Hypnotic Headline

Because hypnotic copywriting does not come naturally, you must get started on it right away so that you can practice immediately and start to build your hypnotic muscle. Remember, you cannot build muscle while watching me. You must do the work to get the desired result.

Think of your website's homepage. Think of the audience that you want to attract. Ask yourself *What is it that I'm really selling?*

Now grab a piece of paper and create at least three hypnotic headlines for your website homepage. Remember, your goal is to capture their attention, hook their interest, and create curiosity. Once you've written your three headlines, bounce them off co-workers or colleagues who will give you some feedback.

Your company name is not a headline. Take the best of your new headlines, after you've shared it with your colleagues, and put it in the prime real estate position of your homepage. Yes, this may be new to you, but I can assure you that this can be one of the most valuable uses of your time today. So go ahead, get your writing started! If you come up with a great headline that you believe is truly world-class material, please share it with me. I'd love to hear it.

Chapter 26—Whale Training

Have you ever been to SeaWorld or seen any aquatic mammal shows? In them, a human, just like you or me, somehow wills a being thousands of pounds heavier than themselves to do things like take them for a ride around the pool, leap high into the air, or splash the crowd with its tail. How on earth do they manage that? Shouldn't the whale be in charge? It all seems so far-fetched, but it happens every day.

Just like people learn step-by-step, whales need to be walked through the learning process, too. The first step, upon introducing a new whale into a pool, is to place a rope along the bottom of the pool so that it effectively cuts the pool area in half. If the whale swims on, for instance, the left side of the rope/pool, the whale doesn't get any food. However, as soon as the whale crosses the rope, it is greeted with fishy treats. Then, if it continues to swim on *that* side of the pool, it will not get fed until it crosses the rope to the *other* side of the pool. Get it? After a few short months, the whale learns its first trick: how to cross a rope.

Crossing the rope is the whale's trigger to get food. The next step is to raise the rope to mid-depth between the top and the bottom of the pool. If the whale swims on, for instance, the left side of the rope or under the rope, then it gets no food, but as soon as the whale swims over the rope to the right side, it is rewarded by being fed. A few months later, after several hundred repetitions, the trainers raise the rope from mid-depth to the surface of the pool. If the whale swims from side to side or under the rope, again, the whale will not be fed. So the whale learns pretty quickly to break the surface of the water and move over the rope. As soon as it does that, it is rewarded. You get the picture: this natural progression continues until the rope is ten to twenty feet in the air. When the whale performs these feats, a whistle is also blown to act as a future trigger of this act. Soon enough, you have a whale that will leap into the air at the sound of a whistle and gesture of its trainer.

People learn in much the same way whales do—step by step. However, in my experience, all too often people try to skip over the interim steps and go directly to the big tricks. People often start businesses before learning how to manage themselves, and end up making poor financial decisions due to inexperience. They enter into presentation situations without learning how to make a presentation successful, and they end up switching from one idea to the next, generally making all kinds of trial-and-error mistakes in situations that call for expertise and precision. Trial and error is easily the most popular learning method, but that doesn't mean that it is effective or timely.

It always amazes me to see people make the same mistakes over and over again and never reach out for the proper help or training. Is it pride that keeps them from seeking out information? Is it ego? Is it because they know it all and nobody can tell them what to do? Whatever the reason, most people try to leap over the rope that's twenty feet in the air without the proper training or information.

Why are people in such a hurry? It seems that everyone wants to go through the local drive-thru and order up success with the side of a big bag of money without having to cook it up themself.

Success comes in stages. When you give it the time that it takes, you will actually enjoy the process. When you try to speed it up, you will actually make mistakes and push yourself backwards. I've mentioned before that one of the quickest ways to get where you want is to stop figuring out how you will get there. All you need to do is take advice and training from someone who is already there—someone who has what you want. If you take advice from people in the same tax bracket, you likely won't become wealthy. If you truly commit to wealth then you must learn step-by-step information from someone who has completed the steps and knows exactly how to steer you clear from the pitfalls so you can avoid the mistakes and move quicker to your goal.

Also, there's something to be said about not rushing a good thing. If you try to leap over the steps and go directly to the finish line, you end up depriving yourself of the experience, the journey, the lessons, and the fun that come with being a successful person. Learning is a very enjoyable experience. However, most people want to skip the learning part and go directly to success because, as I say, most people are in a hurry. What they don't know is that learning and experience are required for success.

Did you know that 99 percent of the creative process is complete before you see any evidence of it in your physical reality? Just as people are about to see the fruits of their labour, they begin to doubt and often give up, only to go back and start all over again, making the same mistakes ad infinitum. But why? Because most people give up just before getting the results they've been seeking. Impatience is the killer of success.

Lesson—Let's Talk About Your Own Training

Let's simplify things down to their basic elements: Like the whale, there is one thing standing between you and success, and that's training.

You can read books, go through trial and error, and witness what other people do and copy. Or, you can train. To train is to learn by doing. It is the essence of Suggestology. When you learn step by step, you build your learning muscles. Common sense dictates that if you are going to learn to play the piano then you will have to learn it step by step. Why should business be any different? Why should success be any different?

It's not.

Of course, I may be a bit impartial towards training because I own and operate a training company, but there's a reason why I own that training company: I got here by investing in my own training. And each time I have invested in myself, my return on the investment has been shocking.

In the past five years I have invested at least once a year in high-level hands-on training courses. I feed my brain a steady diet of nonfiction books, online study courses, and attend conferences and tradeshows like they're going extinct tomorrow. Of course, do your due diligence when it comes to which products to invest in. I make sure to be smart about what I invest in. I can tell you that whether it's internet marketing information or presentation training, I have taken away something valuable from every learning experience I've come to.

Without a doubt, the most valuable type of training that I have ever invested in is personal development, or personal growth, seminars. There is nothing comparable to learning and experiencing high-powered information designed specifically to motivate you from within. Things like learning the natural laws of the universe and believing in the power of manifestation are paramount to your success.

When was the last time you invested in your own personal growth? And if you haven't, what does that say about how much you value your own growth? Are you afraid that your ego will suffer because there exists information that you don't know about yet? Are you worried what others will think of you? Are you fearful that, if you start achieving success, your friends won't like you anymore? Personal growth seminars are designed to retool your thinking processes and get you supercharged emotionally, mentally, physically, and spiritually.

When people hear the word spirituality, they often think religion. It does not have to be that way. Think of spirituality as learning and believing in *universal law*. Things like the law of attraction, the law of detachment, and the law of allowing are there to support you in achieving your desires. Many people are afraid to even consider this as a possibility. For those who reject these laws, it is usually a case of passing judgment on something you likely know nothing about. Understanding spirituality is simply a question of learning step-by-step information about how to achieve success and implementing it that same way—step by step. The way you think and feel about achieving the things that you want in your life are spiritual concepts. And whether or not you believe or understand these concepts, they are still working to

I have taken countless personal growth seminars from master achievers the likes of Tony Robbins, T Harv Ecker, Blair Singer, Brian Klemmer, and more. Yes, in the beginning of my transformation, I was skeptical. Still, I quickly realized that much of what I was learning from these masters was not only easily understandable but also easy to implement. A lot of their stuff is about daily actions that you can take to attract and manifest the life that you want. Most people discount the concept of personal growth because they feel that somehow they are above it or too smart for it. Figure that out—too smart for personal growth! Hah!

Somehow they feel that it's too corny or that it can't possibly be true. Based on what? What your friends tell you? Sure, your friends may laugh at you when you tell them you're going to a personal growth seminar. I can tell you that a few of my friends from my old life think I'm completely nuts. Yet I'm the one whose financial situation has increased exponentially; I'm the one with the two-million-dollar home and big white motor yacht! I'm the one who has guided over 20,000 people towards their own success. It's so much easier for you to talk badly about someone else than it is to actually do something about your own situation. Isn't it? But guess what? The successful friends who I have now? They wouldn't laugh at you for going to a personal growth seminar—they would respect you. That goes to show you that richness is not just a money thing but a mind frame, as well. The friends who you have now—would they support your goals of self-improvement or laugh them away? If you find that friends are holding you back, choking you with their complaints, bringing you down with their sad and miserable energy or constantly blaming the world for their problems, isn't it time you took a breather from that kind of energy and experienced a personal growth seminar? I can tell you that the energy in one of these seminars is incredible.

If you're not sure about where to go for a personal growth seminar, and you need some direction or guidance then might I suggest one of our highest rated seminars entitled, "Agents Of Change." Training Business Pros is known primarily as a business-to-business marketing training company. Our specialties are Internet marketing, social media, affiliate marketing, e-commerce, presentation marketing, trade show and conference marketing. It is only in the past year that I have introduced the course, "Agents Of Change." This was a significant risk on our part. Our fear was; how would people perceive us? We did not want to be labeled just another personal development company. However, my feeling is; just like Brian Klemmer says, "If how-to's were enough we all be skinny rich and happy." It's more than just how-to's.

Success will continue to elude you if you don't have intrinsic motivation, energy, and spiritual wakefulness. I noticed in my business training courses that, even though I'm giving people amazing how-to information, often times I will see them months later and they will give me excuses as to why they hadn't implemented the information. In the case of internet marketing, my information about search engine optimization could essentially help you and your company make millions of dollars. Why would you postpone the implementation process?

That is why I developed the Agents of Change seminar—so that you could become an agent of change in your life and in the lives of others. If you help someone get what they want first, then you will have what they have in abundance. As an agent of change, you will learn the same powerful secrets as hundreds of public speakers, authors, corporate leaders, politicians, and medical professionals who use these methods every day to infuse powerful change in other people's lives and fuel their purpose-driven lives.

Do you want to master the ability to create deep, long-lasting change in-group situations? Experience the kind of change that explodes productivity, fires up creativity, and gets you monumental results in a short period of time. You will be offered specialized techniques extracted from marketing and behavioural research disciplines to help you harness key critical skills and master your leadership skills. Whether you're in a boardroom, a training session, a conference, or a sales meeting, you will never fail to earn the trust, credibility, and respect of the group you are steering. You will learn powerful ways to help others to take meaningful action in their lives while living with integrity within your personal belief systems.

Here's what you will learn:

how to adopt the rules for learning (accountability, the willingness to accept guidance, participation and energy);

why most people settle for what they have even though they want more, and how you can shift your focus away from average;

how to practice the law of attraction on a daily basis, which will allow you to focus on and attain what you want;

how to remove limiting beliefs and adopt empowering beliefs that lead to new habits;

how to recognize *lack* mentality in your thought processes and how to cancel it out in favour of *abundance* mentality;

how to become a deliberate creator by focusing on your message and your purpose for others;

how to ask the world's most powerful questions like world-class coaches do to ignite purpose, direction, and results in their teams and/or clients;

how to create a binding agreement between yourself and the universe that will immediately activate positive change and results;

what your emotional guidance system is and how you can use it to stay on track;

how to communicate with your ESP (Essential Silent Partner), make requests on a regular basis, and have them fulfilled.

how to create multiple daily actions in your life that will attract more money, opportunity, and abundance.

how to understand the laws of flow and create positive actions as a result;

how to figure out what it is you truly desire;

how to create powerful intentions that will activate the achievement of your desires;

how to create deep commitment in your life once and for all so that are competing intentions will not get in the way of your success.

how to practice the law of detachment and the law of allowing so that your life will flow with abundance and peace;

how to practice Suggestology so that you can engage people as a true leader and agent of change;

how to become a super persuader by understanding the five action steps to ensure success in any situation;

how to read people fast: 4 Behaviour modes that could help you become a master communicator in any situation;

advanced NLP techniques that will decrease resistance and help you handle objections with ease;

key body communication skills (What your body gestures may be saying that you may not be aware of);

how your voice, pitch, tempo, and power can damage your leadership potential, so that you can learn "command" mode or "friendly power" by improving one simple part of your leadership style; and how to utilize Intention Mechanisms and Deep Commitment to help your team make life-changing decisions and create explosive results!

There is a big difference between reading information and practicing it. What you hear, you tend to forget. What you see or read, you tend to remember. But what you do, you understand! There is nothing like working through exercises with a master trainer to help you assimilate information by understanding each and every aspect of the implementation process. That's what the Agents of Change seminar has been shaped to help you do.

It is always very important to get supporting evidence when deciding in what seminar to invest. Here are some recent testimonials from graduates of the Agents of Change seminar:

"I enjoyed the opportunity to set goals and to make some action plans. You helped me to realize I have to let go of things—to clear out things will allows new things to come into my life. It was also a great opportunity to meet all of the people who took the course. Thank you."

- Debbie Milner, QuickBooks Consultant and internet Marketer @ eBiz Support Services

"Excellent program. Did not want it to end even though it was tiring."

- Christopher Chin, Manager – Marketing and Special Events @ Atlas Tire Wholesale Inc.

"What a great course/workshop/seminar. Agents of Change brings the purpose of your work to light. I can't wait to apply the tools that I've learned this weekend and learn more throughout my life."

- Ian McIntosh, Fun Meister @ Barrie Social Club

"Becoming an 'Agent of Change' has made me more accountable to my desires. I can't let Paul Tobey down, so change is the only way. During this course I have found what limited me, and I'm on my way to a better me. I now have a clearer vision (desire) and way to manifest the outcomes. I may not know the road I will take, but I know I will get there through intent and being a deliberate creator. There are no longer any limitations."

"A life changing experience that gave me the opportunity to discover a very worthwhile goal and purpose to move towards that while both helping myself and those who I want to positively affect. It gave me the tools to get there."

- Michael Schart, Photographer @ MJS Photography

"I feel empowered with new tools and techniques to make a positive impact in the world and build the life I truly desire."

- Nancy Mayer, Management Consultant

To register for your 3-hour free preview of the "Agents of Change" seminar visit this URL today:

http://www.trainingbusinesspros.com/m/agents-of-change

Exercise—Live By The Calendar

When you pick goals you should always pick a deadline in which to frame them. It fosters commitment and motivation when you put a limitation on the amount of time you give yourself to create your goal. Your goal for this exercise is to seek out a training course and mark your calendar as to when you will attend. It all starts with the date. If you do not commit to a date, then you are not deeply committed to change. There is a saying: Don't put off until tomorrow what you can do today. Make today the day that you commit to change by marking in your calendar the cut-off date as to when you register and participate in a personal growth or professional development seminar.

At the risk of sounding repetitive (even though repetition can be the key to initiating some empowering behaviours!), I cannot emphasize enough the value that personal growth seminars and professional development seminars have played in my own life and personal success. Every time I invest in myself, I get a significant return on that investment. Likewise, training is possibly the only thing that stands between you and what you want.

I was resistant to change for many years. Now that I have received the proper training, however, I only see opportunity. And because I see opportunity I learn how to harness it, ride it, experience it, and create it for others and myself. I needed to be trained.

Perhaps you need it, too? What would your life look like if, with the proper training, you knew you couldn't fail? It is possible to not fail. However, learning step-by-step on how to create the mindset (and the heart set) that will guide you towards success takes a decision on your part. When is the day that you decide to change?

There is only now.

In the end, all of this comes down to what kind of life you want. If you are content and peaceful and financially successful in your current life, then you most likely know that life is a great experiment and you will seek out more information to continue to learn and grow. More often than not, it is people who are unhappy, fearful, broke, miserable, and resistant to change who never invest in themselves. Somehow they feel that life will change without learning or taking action. That's impossible. Even if you feel that this is not the right time for you—which, by the way, it *is*—try to remember the following two rules:

Never take advice from people who do not have what you want; and

Make sure that others benefit from your actions.

If you follow these two rules, it is the beginning of a new life for you. You will no longer sit and complain about the poor state of affairs your finances are in, and you most likely will not want to hear it from your friends, either. You will become goal-oriented. My wish for you is that you look back on your life without regret; that you prosper through a series of successes that span your lifetime and beyond.

When you let go of the safety of the trapeze bar you currently swing from, you will learn to fly. In fact, you have already poised yourself for the jump by reading this book.

Flying is fun. It's exciting, enjoyable, peaceful, motivational, enthusiastic, full of learning, packed with discovery, and supercharged with opportunity, but only when you learn to fly. You already have an incredible advantage having read this book; you are obviously open to changing your life for the better and inspired to let go of your limiting beliefs. Today's the day. Set a cut-off date. Commit to letting go. Learn to fly, and I'll see you in the sky.

About the Author

Paul Tobey, CEO, Training Business Pros

After a 20 year multi-award winning career as a jazz pianist and recording artist with Arkadia Records, Paul Tobey switched from artistry to entrepreneurship and began to take on the world of Internet marketing. His reputation as a world-class marketer grew quickly through the sale of sheet music and online video piano lessons and branched out into other information driven websites focused on helping businesses and entrepreneurs.

After exiting the music performance business, walking across Spain and a brief mentoring period with some of the world's top trainers, Tobey founded Training Business Pros and is now considered by industry peers as one of North America's top trainers. He has personally trained thousands of business owners, business executives, public speakers, trainers, realtors, financial advisors, mortgage brokers, sales teams and internet marketing specialists; helping them earn hundreds of thousands of dollars and save on their bottom line.